THE STORY OF THE FLY AND HOW IT COULD SAVE THE WORLD

PUBLISHER Cheviot Publishing cc
DESIGNER Catherine Coetzer COVER DESIGN Katrin Hannusch
EDITORS Melissa Siebert and Guy Harrison
PRINTING & BINDING CTP Printers (South Africa), CPI Ltd (United Kingdom)

First edition published in 2012 by Cheviot Publishing cc

Printed on FSC certified paper

Cheviot Publishing cc Reg. No. 2005/010348/23
PO Box 15096, Vlaeberg 8018, South Africa
www.cheviot-publishing.com
Printed edition ISBN 978-0-9802742-8-8

DEDICATION

This book is dedicated to the trillions of flies that will give up their lives to save our seas and help feed humanity in the 21st Century.

It's the least we can do.

ACKNOWLEDGEMENTS

This work brings together the detailed research of many international scientists, academics, entomologists and medical doctors over the last 200 years who are too numerous to mention. But of course our gratitude goes to all of them.

We would particularly like to thank Genghis Khan, the legendary Mongol warrior and conqueror, for his early work on flies in medicine. We would also like to thank Dr Elsje Pieterse of Stellenbosch University and David Drew, Roy Rudolphe, Elaine Gloy and Duncan Miller of Agriprotein Technologies for their modern-day research and insights into animal nutrition and *Musca domestica* – the humble housefly with a great future.

Jason Drew and Justine Joseph
July 2012

PROLOGUE

AS A BUSINESSMAN and serial entrepreneur, I have spent the last 25 years of my life working in corporations – running other people's multinational companies, and then creating and selling my own.

Two heart attacks later, I traded the struggles of the boardroom for a passion for life and moved to my farm in South Africa's beautiful Tulbagh valley.

It proved to be a move towards deeper understanding – both of the environment and of myself. It sparked within me a love and concern for our planet. I then travelled the world to see for myself the damage that we are wreaking on the vital ecosystems on which we depend. Before this journey into the environment, I understood neither the unbelievable risks we are taking, nor the extraordinary opportunities for entrepreneurs and eco-capitalists like myself.

Following that journey of discovery, I wrote my first book with David Lorimer, *The Protein Crunch – Civilisation on the Brink*. I looked at the environment as I saw it, from the perspective of an unashamed capitalist and entrepreneur. As we move out of the era of the Industrial Revolution and into the Sustainability Revolution, capitalists and environmentalists will become natural bedfellows, not the adversaries they once were in the old world order.

I have also become fascinated by and optimistic about the many extraordinary things that individuals and companies around the world are doing to help fix our future. I, too, have since become involved by supporting, starting and investing in some various amazing green businesses.

In 2009, I found myself following a trail of industrial agricultural production from 40,000 cows in air-conditioned sheds in Saudi to a chicken farm and abattoir in the Western Cape, South Africa.

I met the slaughterhouse owner and followed the process through to the lake of blood behind the abattoir, around it millions of flies (buzzing in F-minor). It occurred to me that it takes as much water, land and fuel to produce the bits of a chicken that we throw away as it does to produce the bits we eat. And we throw away a lot.

The slaughterhouse owner told me that he had had a visit the previous week from a scientist who was looking into recycling the waste from that abattoir using flies. I was intrigued, and pleased to be introduced to Dr Elsje Pieterse, Head of Animal Nutrition at Stellenbosch University. And so began my love affair with flies.

I spent the next year researching and developing the business with my brother David and close friends and business partners Roy Rudolphe and Duncan Miller. The business, called AgriProtein Technologies, now run by my brother, has industrialised the process of rearing fly larvae on waste nutrients, effectively recycling them into a high-quality natural feed. It is, after all, what chickens in the fields and fish in the streams would naturally eat. The aim is to replace fishmeal in industrial farming with larvae meal. It has been a challenging and amazing process, resulting in AgriProtein building its firs commercial-scale plant in 2012.

We take it for granted that we need to recycle our paper, glass and tin. It will become increasingly evident that we also need to recycle waste nutrients, whether it be food waste from supermarkets or abattoir waste from industrial slaughterhouses.

I have seen the beginnings of waste nutrient recycling in Thailand, where catfish are grown in raw human sewerage. The mature fish are then taken to a clear stream 100 kilometres from Bangkok where, after six weeks, they are clean of all impurities and delivered to the city's restaurants where the cycle starts again.

While we are perhaps not yet ready for this seemingly unpleasant nutrient-recycling loop, it is still certain that recycling human sewerage and other waste nutrient sources will be commonplace industries in the 21st Century. In fact, if humanity is to survive without the starvation that has marked human history until the last 50 years, it will most likely be a necessity.

The Story of the Fly and How It Could Save the World is the fascinating, previously unwritten story of a remarkable creature that has always been part of daily human life. As we were researching the insect and its life cycle in order to build our business, we came across some extraordinary facts about the fly that we had to share with those of you who still see these bugs only as a nuisance.

Hopefully, this book will change your mind. Hopefully, you will start to see the fly not as a pain in the neck, but as the potential saviour of our planet and our seas. It's clear that this insect deserves our respect – it was, after all, the first animal (after the human) to have its genome sequenced.

In due course, hopefully the fly will join fish, pigs, chickens, sheep and cows as the sixth and probably the most numerous industrially farmed animal on the planet. It's a goal worth reaching for. It could help save the world.

Jason Drew

CONTENTS

CHAPTER 1

THE STORY BEGINS

CAN YOU KEEP A FLY AS A PET? It's a strange question. An even stranger one might be: Would you really want to?

But if your desire is firm and fly petting is your thing, the answer to both questions is a strange and certain 'yes'. Of course you can keep a fly as a pet. If you can catch it, that is.

Swatting is easy enough – more than 200 wing beats per second translate to a speed of only 7.5 kilometres per hour, about that of a brisk human walk. That said, trapping an unsuspecting housefly using an overturned tumbler or, if you're really good, two rapidly cupped hands, will most likely require many, mostly futile, attempts. If and when you do catch it, you'll need to bring your new pet to heel.

That's the thing about houseflies. They fly around a lot, which makes them difficult to train, or at the very least attach to a leash. But it can be done. Fly fundis, clearly as brutal as they are bored, will advise you to pop your fly into a plastic container and stick it in the fridge for a few minutes (or maybe it's the freezer; they can't quite agree). This will cool and calm it down to almost a standstill. Then you can take it out, dazed and confused but still very much alive, and tie a piece of string or dental floss around its body. A long human hair can work well too. That's if the pet fly thing isn't strange enough for you already.

Finally, you tie the other end of the floss, hair or string to a heavy object like a spoon or paperweight. And there you have it: your very own pet fly, fit for hours of obediently circling. It's a great way to spend a lazy Sunday afternoon. A YouTube video waiting to happen.

In the interest of good personal hygiene and insect welfare, you would probably be ill-advised to try this at home. Plus a housefly would not make a good pet. On the contrary, it's built to be a bad one. Whether tied to a string or trapped in a cosy kitchen container, it won't last more than a couple of days in captivity. And, even if it does, at a centimetre in length and weighing approximately 12 milligrams, it's way too small to be scratched under the chin or stroked. A fly generally goes out of its way to avoid being touched by anything at all, even a gust of wind. And if it were more amenable to fun, games and affection, the bacteria it carries would be even more of a problem.

After examining almost 400,000 houseflies, a pair of Chinese entomologists concluded that a single fly carries more than 1.9 million bacteria.

After examining almost 400,000 houseflies – an unenviable task to be sure – Doctors Yao Hong-Wei and Yuan De-cheng, Chinese entomologists from Zhejiang University, Hangzhou, concluded that a single fly carries more than 1.9 million bacteria. That is some serious baggage. In fact, flies are thought to be responsible for more human deaths than humans are responible for fly deaths. Which, if you consider the booming bug spray and flytrap industries, is a lot (and a very good reason to avoid flies like the plague).

Clearly, a fly can be kept as a pet, but you probably don't want one after all. Why? Because pets are meant to improve your quality of life in some way and flies just don't. Mostly they spend their time turning up in soup, irritating Australians (who had to invent the cork-rimmed hat to deal with them), landing on all kinds of garbage and generally making life not better, but worse. It's no wonder they have never been domesticated. It's no wonder no one has ever even tried.

This is certainly not for a lack of time. Flies are thought to have existed on Earth for more than 20 million years – about 19.5 million more than any form of human life. Their ancestors probably pestered our ancestors. Our ancestors probably fashioned rudimentary flyswats out of leaves. And it's been interspecies war ever since.

We try to kill them, they try to kill us, and despite countless casualties on either side, no one's really winning. In fact, it all seems rather futile. Especially if you consider the fact that we might be able to combine our talents to do something good. Like saving the world.

Because it does need saving, and it's all our fault.

Honey catches more flies than vinegar, so let me say this as sweetly as I can. If the Earth is a great big picnic blanket laid out for all living things, the flies aren't the ones walking all over the potato salad with their dirty little feet. The humans are the real pests at this picnic called life. In addition to the way we pump out waste (something the flies might thank us for if no one else does), we also have a tendency to eat, drink and merrily use up natural resources like there is no tomorrow. Until tomorrow comes, of course. Which it always does in the end.

Consider the fish in the ocean. Because of our actions, they are dropping like, well, flies. Actually it's because of our actions and our appetites – and not just our appetite for the fish themselves. It all comes down to protein. Humans really want and need protein. Technically, we need it because it plays a structural and functional role in every cell, as well as in the membranes, enzymes and hormones that keep things running. Not so technically, we also like protein because it tastes good – particularly the kind that comes from animals.

A quick biology lesson: Protein is made up of amino acid building blocks. Although the body can manufacture certain of these amino acids in-house, nine have to be provided by our diet. These are called the essential or indispensable amino acids. Their indispensability is what makes some proteins more valuable than others.

Animal proteins like meat, poultry, fish, eggs and dairy products provide enough of all nine essential amino acids to earn the title complete proteins. But plant proteins, like those in vegetables and other plants as well as nuts and seeds, don't. That's why they are called incomplete proteins and need to be combined with others (or with man-made versions of the missing amino acids) to deliver the right cocktail of amino acids to promote growth in monogastric (single-stomached) animals like fish, poultry, pigs, dogs, cats and, of course, humans.

The same does not apply to ruminants – like cattle, goats and sheep – that have multi-chambered stomachs, chew the cud and use a stepwise, ultra-efficient digestive process to squeeze every bit of energy out of the grain or grass they are fed. They can do fine on a diet of plants. They don't need the above-mentioned cocktail of amino acids for their protein kick. But monogastric animals (let's call them monogasts for short) do. In fact, monogasts like us need a very particular protein mix – and it starts with the kind that's complete.

Clearly, getting enough protein is a human health priority. But how much is enough? According to the Food and Nutrition Board at the US National Academy of Sciences' Institute of Medicine in Washington, DC, Recommended Daily Allowance (RDA) or Adequate Intake (AI) for an adult is 46 to 56 grams of preferably complete protein per day, or 10 to 35 percent of total calories consumed. That's about equal to one small piece of steak or tin of tuna. But most of us probably want more than that. Some experts estimate that the average American eats double their protein RDA every day.

Like it, want it or need it, complete protein is an integral part of the monogastric diet. We humans take this very seriously. That's why we are very serious about eating protein in the form of dairy products, eggs and, even more so, animals. Lots and lots of animals for the lots and lots of people that populate the planet. And there are more and more of us by the day. Statistics show that humans are in fact responsible for 100 million acts of sexual intercourse every day – that's according to 2011 research by Durex (who better to ask?). The World Health Organisation (WHO) says this leads to about 374,000 births per day, which – if you subtract the 170,000 deaths –means that 204,000 more people sit down for supper every

There are 100 million acts of human sexual intercourse every day. There are also 374,000 births and 170,000 deaths, which means that 204,000 more people sit down for supper every evening than had breakfast that morning. That's a lot more mouths to feed.

evening than had breakfast that morning. That's like adding the population of New York City to the world every month. It's impressive procreation. But also a lot more mouths to feed.

You see, humans are survivalists. We are very good at finding ways to survive – mainly by thinking up new ways to eat more, build better shelters, have more children and dodge more diseases. We are successfully turning the diverse biomass of the planet into human biomass. How do we produce the number of animals required to feed our ever-growing population's ever-growing need? Industrially, that's how.

Industrial farming is both a boon and a blight. It allows us to produce vast amounts of affordable beef, chicken, pork, eggs and fish. It helps us generate more protein in less time. It's controllable, reproducible and super-marketable – a way to deliver the right food at the right time to our supermarkets, at a price we can afford. But, industrial farming is not very sustainable, particularly animal farming. You have to put in lots of energy and protein to get out not very much of the optimal protein.

Industrial animal farming is not sustainable. Mostly because you have to put lots of energy and protein in to get not very much of the optimal protein out.

But it's not just us. All animals need protein. Industrially farmed monogasts need complete proteins that deliver all the necessary amino acids in the correct amounts. This generally comes from one of two sources: the land or the sea. Soya from the land is 30 percent protein by volume, but it's plant protein and therefore `incomplete'. This means it's a less convenient animal feed that needs to be supplemented with additional man-made amino acids. Fishmeal from the sea is 52 percent animal protein and complete. This might be more convenient, but it's far from a sustainable solution. In fact, generating sustainable amounts of either protein is something of an environmental juggling act. As the human population and hunger for protein explode, it's no wonder we are dropping balls.

Soya production demands enormous quantities of water, land and fossil fuel for transport and fertiliser. Fishmeal production, obviously, calls for enormous quantities of fish. That's the problem: dwindling natural resources and a growing global demand have driven up the price of both protein sources significantly. But the financial cost is small change when compared to the environmental costs. Especially when it comes to fishmeal.

Fish farming or aquaculture needs 2.3 kg of fish to produce 1 kg of fish, only 30 percent of which is consumed by humans – the fillets. The rest is waste.

If it doesn't end up in our pet food, about 30 percent of all the fish caught from the ocean ends up on industrial farms being fed to chickens, pigs, prawns, shrimp and other fish. In fact, even efficient fish farming or aquaculture operations need 2.3 kg of fish to produce 1 kg of farmed fish, only 30 percent of which is ultimately consumed by humans – the fillets. The rest is waste. And that really is a waste. It's something like a 200 percent protein investment for a 30 percent yield. You don't need to be an economist to see that this is a recipe for bankruptcy. And that's exactly what's happening in our seas: not a credit crunch, but a protein crunch.

A quick ecology lesson: Greenpeace estimates that our global fishing capacity is now four times greater than there are fish left to catch sustainably. The United Nations agrees, saying that more than 70 percent of the world's fisheries are 'over exploited,' 'fully exploited,' or 'significantly depleted'. This is unsurprising, considering that the UN Food and Agriculture Organization (FAO) 2010 review estimates that 145 million tonnes of fish were eaten in 2009. Of this, 55 million tonnes were farmed and 90 million tonnes were caught at sea. According to the review, '115 million tonnes was used as human food, providing an estimated apparent per capita supply of about 17 kg (live weight equivalent), which is an all-time high.'

The report shows that aquaculture is the fastest-growing animal-food-producing sector. In fact, it's getting fast enough to outpace our very fast-paced population growth. Per capita fish supply from aquaculture alone went from 0.7 kg in 1970 to 7.8 kg in 2008, an average annual growth rate of 6.6 percent. It's more than a ten-fold increase overall.

A rhino horn will sell for around $440,000. A single blue-fin tuna sold for a record $736 234 at a January 2012 fish auction in Tokyo.

The big, scary numbers just get bigger and scarier. Nearly 30 percent of all the fish we take from our oceans is used in industrial and farming operations. Now, more than 90 percent of large predatory fish like cod and tuna is gone. In January 2012, at the first fish auction of the year in Tokyo, a single blue-fin tuna sold for a record $736,234. Granted, the fish weighed 296 kg and was bought for high-quality sushi meat. But, if you consider that a rhino horn will fetch merely half that amount on the illegal black market (around $440,000), the scarcity of fish species that were previously staples begins to swim into focus. That's why other species now have to be targeted – which has led to some creative rebranding by the fishing industry. The Slimehead is now known as the more appetising Orange Roughy and the Patagonian Toothfish as the tastier-sounding Chilean Seabass.

And then there is the krill fishing.

Krill are small, pink, shrimp-like crustaceans that eat phytoplankton and are eaten by bigger marine animals, such as fish, seals, whales and penguins. Because these larger animals don't eat plankton themselves, the krill constitute an essential link in the aquatic food chain. Now they are also becoming essential to aquaculture. Why? Because there are fewer fish available to feed to more fish farms than ever before.

Over 75 percent of the world's fish oil and 40 percent of its fishmeal currently goes into aquaculture, say estimates from within the fishing industry. Most farmed fish and shrimp need complete animal protein to keep going and growing. But clearly, at this rate, the supply of wild fish cannot continue to meet the industry's fishmeal demand. The next lowest complete animal protein in the marine food chain is krill. So krill oil and meal will just have to do. Conveniently, these feeds are also high in protein, low in pollutants and can help to give farmed salmon its famous colour (boosted by pink dye of various shades). The industry is happy enough to make the change. But the marine ecosystem isn't.

The greatest population of krill is found in the Southern Ocean around Antarctica. As the fishing industry turns its attention to this area, so too do the conservationists. A report in the February 2011 issue of Fishing and Fisheries stated that, for the 17 years leading up to 2009, Antarctic krill fishing was stable at about 120,000 tonnes a year. Since then it's increased to more than 200,000 tonnes, an amount that's expanding as fish stocks continue to decline.

Let's face it - we have eaten from the top of the marine food chain towards the bottom. The insatiable human hunger for resources strikes again. When we get to the bottom it's game over – for the oceans and for us. It's no wonder that the Pew Environment Group's Antarctic Krill Conservation Project, part of the Washington, DC-based charitable foundation, says that shrinking krill populations could place the entire Antarctic ecosystem at risk. Research has shown that even localised krill loss can hamper penguin, whale and seal populations. Imagine what it could do on an oceanwide scale.

With enough awareness and planning, the krill crisis may yet be averted. But, when it comes to over-fishing, it could be too late to stem the tide. The regulation of fishing and vessels is lagging pitifully behind the accelerating problem. In 2007 the US-based sustainability foundation, the Worldwatch Institute, in its report, Oceans in Peril: Protecting Marine Biodiversity, ventured that our only option may be to declare 40 percent of the oceans off limits for fishing. This will probably never happen, although in 2002 the UN agreed that by 2012, 10 percent of all oceans should be declared marine reserves in order to protect our fish stocks. Politicians have yet again failed to deliver on their own promises. Nevertheless, with or without restrictions, we have to go ever further and ever deeper to catch the same amount of fish. And this, of course, leads to ever-increasing costs.

In 2006 it took about one litre of diesel to catch one kg of fish. Now it takes two litres of diesel, which itself is ever more expensive due to rising fuel prices. If we want to keep generating enough protein to support the human need, we simply must find something more sustainable to support the process. A new complete protein source desperately needs to be found - one that costs less than fishmeal, both economically and environmentally.

Sustainable aquaculture, according to Greenpeace, involves monitoring both what you put in and what you take out. The input shouldn't lead to the depletion of natural resources, or use fishmeal or fish-oil feeds from unsustainable fisheries. Similarly, the output shouldn't result in environmental damage or a net loss in fish protein yield. That's why sustainability-conscious fish farmers are being pushed towards using to use plant-based feeds that are sustainably grown – at least for mainly vegetarian fish (like tilapia or barramundi), if not for carnivorous, protein-eating salmon and trout.

Switching to plant feeds like soya is not an ideal solution. Firstly, its production comes with its own costs and challenges, and secondly, soya protein is incomplete as it is missing certain vital amino acids in the protein mix. This means that farmed poultry and pigs that are fed soya need a side-order of additional man-made amino acids to make their protein supply complete. Fish like salmon and trout, and crustaceans like prawns, can't be grown on this artificial mix. They need animal protein with its higher concentration of complete protein to grow successfully. Clearly, it's a conundrum: the animal protein we need is not sustainable, while the plant protein we get is not quite interchangeable and just won't work in aquaculture.

But what if sustainability could be achieved with another kind of animal protein? What if that protein was complete, but also completely sustainable? What if this protein could be generated using waste products from the animal industry itself? Well, it can. But, again, it depends on what you put in and what you take out.

The search for sustainable farming calls for a bit of recycling. In this case it's nutrient recycling – using free waste products to generate valuable food products.

In any industry, the search for a better input-output balance calls for a bit of recycling. In this case it's nutrient recycling – using `free', existing waste products to generate valuable food products. The key is finding something to do that regenerating, and it helps if that something is built to do the job.

Which brings us back to the fly, more specifically *Musca domestica*, the common housefly. It really is one of the most common insects worldwide. It's found on every continent in every environment and it multiplies in massive numbers to keep things that way. The housefly is a survivalist. In short, it's just like us. It's an excellent breeder – a female will lay up to 800 eggs in her lifetime, usually in some kind of warm organic material or waste. These eggs hatch into larvae, which take just a few days to increase over 400 times in weight. Unless they are eaten before that.

Fish and birds love to eat flies and larvae. Chickens will naturally peck around in the dirt for them and fish will jump out of streams to grab at them. Why? Because larvae are protein powerhouses. Nutritionally speaking, they are more natural than and at least as good as fishmeal. And when it comes to soya, they are more sustainable and certainly more complete. You can see where this is going. Waste plus flies equals larvae plus protein.

> Fish and birds love to eat flies and larvae. Chickens naturally peck around in the dirt for them and fish will jump out of streams to grab at them. Why? Because larvae are protein powerhouses.

This kind of organic alchemy was first attempted in 1919 when a biologist named Lindner started tinkering around with houseflies and human waste. His rather off-putting study involved feeding sewage to fly larvae and watching them grow. And it worked – the larvae thrived. But instead of being allowed to turn into pupae, the larvae were harvested, dried and converted into a useful protein source. Although no one knew quite how useful.

Research into flies and their lifecycle reached new highs in Europe during the 1930s and 1940s – driven mostly by wartime fears and food security concerns. Then in 1969 three researchers at Ohio State University in Columbus, Ohio – CC Calvert, RD Martin and NO Morgan – used poultry waste and houseflies to generate their own dried fly pupae protein. This they fed to baby chicks for their first two weeks of life. The conclusion: this fly-generated feed contained enough high-quality protein to support normal growth and development. A triumph for the research trio, but one that was still never actively pursued. The economics of production at the time didn't add up.

It makes sense. Flies like waste and animals like flies. Therefore, if waste from the animal protein industry – like blood and offcuts from abattoirs – can be fuel for flies, then fly larvae can be an efficient fuel for the animals in the fish and meat industry itself. It's a sustainable circle. A self-supporting cycle of nutrients begetting nutrients in a loop.

Nature is full of these circles and loops. One organism's waste is another's favourite food. That's why, in the natural world, everything balances out and so little goes to waste. Perhaps it's time we slotted into this cycle by following a species that's naturally smart and sustainable – like the fly.

One organism's waste is another's favourite food. Perhaps it's time we slotted into the cycle by following a species that's naturally smart and sustainable – like the fly.

Flies may not make great pets, but that doesn't mean they can't improve our lives. Not just agriculturally, but also environmentally, medically, scientifically and even recreationally (which has nothing to do with tying them to a piece of string). That's what this book is about -- seeing flies as much more than they appear to be.

It's time to look a little closer at these alleged pests. It's time to investigate the good, the bad and the ugly. You might be surprised at what you find – more good than bad, and a pretty useful kind of ugly. The fact is, flies are here to stay and we should start appreciating how and why they are here. The truth is, life wouldn't be a picnic without them.

CHAPTER 2

FLY AS ENEMY

IT'S PROBABLY THE MOST FAMOUS fly swat in history. The date: June 2009. The scene: a television interview with CNBC. The swatter: interviewee, US President Barack Obama. The script: 'That was pretty impressive, wasn't it? I got the sucker.' Verbatim.

As the camera swung to the dead fly on the floor, the splat echoed across the world through airwaves, newsfeeds, Internet cables and reporters' over-eager puns. Even People for the Ethical Treatment of Animals (PETA) had something to add.

'Well, I guess it can't be said that President Obama wouldn't hurt a fly,' blogged PETA representative Alisa Mullins. "In a nutshell, our position is this: he isn't the Buddha, he is a human being, and human beings have a long way to go before they think before they act."

'That was pretty impressive, wasn't it? I got the sucker.'
— Barack Obama

Mullins went on to say that PETA was sending a 'humane bug catcher' to Obama, 'for future insect incidents.' It's called the Katcha Bug – a plastic dome with a handle and a clever shutter mechanism. Basically, you place the dome over the fly on a flat surface. Then a quick twist makes the shutter drop and traps the fly inside, unharmed and happy to be released out of the White House front door. Mission accomplished. Insect incident avoided.

Whether or not the President has gone from SWAT team to Katcha Bug is still unknown. What is known, however, is that it wouldn't make a speck of difference either way.

Humans have been squashing, spraying and swishing away flies for all of recorded history. Not without just cause. Flies have been bugging humans for just as long, if not longer. The fourth of the Bible's Ten Plagues was a rampant swarm of flies, and ancient Egyptian hieroglyphics frequently show pharaohs followed closely by court officials armed with fly whisks. Greek mythology also made mention of the pestilent pests – a dedicated god called Myiagros was assigned the role of shooing away flies before sacrifices to Zeus and Athena (clearly not the most important god on the block, but still a job considered worthy of divine intervention).

If humans have been trying to kill flies for as long as the two have shared the planet and hot meals, why are there still so many of them? Truth is, there aren't. At least there aren't as many as there could be.

One pair of flies could easily spawn six to seven generations and 200 quintillion offspring in just five months. If none were killed or eaten, that would be enough to blanket the entire Earth with a layer of flies 47-foot deep.

Left to their own devices, a couple of loved-up flies could easily spawn six to seven generations and 200 quintillion offspring in just five months. There is a bit of debate as to what exactly constitutes a quintillion – in Britain it's a 1 followed by 18 zeroes, and in the US a 1 followed by 30 zeroes (of course everything is bigger and better in the States). But, the number of zeroes aside, scientists estimate that the above-mentioned pair of flies' unchecked breeding would be enough to blanket the entire Earth with a layer of flies 47-foot deep. In only five months! Fortunately, according to research performed by University of California entomologist Fred Legner in the 1960s, this could never happen. Too many animals eat or kill flies – including us – meaning that the insect's population is naturally limited or controlled by about 98 percent.

Bernard Greenberg, international fly authority and professor of biological sciences at the University of Illinois, agrees that fly numbers are reduced by many possible forces. These include natural predators – like birds, reptiles and other insects – as well as a number of environmental factors. In fact, flies and their progeny are very thin-skinned and sensitive when it comes to their surroundings. They need the right supply of the right kind of food.

They need optimal moisture levels and precise temperatures to keep mating, laying eggs, growing rapidly and metamorphosing from egg to larva to pupa to fly.

Temperature is probably the thing they're most pernickety about. Because flies are essentially tropical creatures, they do better when it's warmer. At 10° or 11°C they lose the ability to fly. At 7°C they just about lose consciousness. And at even a touch below freezing they are dead in a couple of hours. They are also dead if the temperature climbs above 46° or 47°C. In fact, they are happiest and most productive (read: reproductive) when it hovers around the low 30s.

But, despite these sensitivities, flies are ubiquitous. The housefly, in particular, is found all over the world. It can survive the harshest winter in the iciest clime, as long as there is a human house, barn, hut or hovel in which to hide out and keep warm. That said, fly fundi Greenberg thinks that Africa is the cradle of both human and fly-kind alike. That's probably why the African continent is home to the largest number of fly species and subspecies. But it's also home to the greatest risk of fly-borne diseases – which brings us to the real reason flies and humans are not likely to stop killing each other any time soon.

The housefly can survive the harshest winter in the iciest clime, as long as there is a human house, barn, hut or hovel in which to hide out and keep warm.

HOW DO FLIES KILL HUMANS?

Dysentery, typhoid, cholera, salmonella, poliomyelitis, tapeworm. Eye infections like trachoma and conjunctivitis. Skin infections like yaws, cutaneous diphtheria and leprosy. It's not a nice list, and not a nice lesson. The lesson is that all these diseases can be picked up and passed on by flies. In fact flies make particularly good taxis for disease-causing organisms on the move. Why? Because they have a taste for both organic waste and human food. A taste that drives them hungrily from dung pile to dinner plate, collecting passengers on one side and delivering them on the other.

No prizes for guessing why someone came up with the term 'filth flies' to describe a group that includes the housefly, blowfly, bottle fly, flesh fly and sometimes the drain fly, fruit fly and phorid fly. Clearly they all like to eat, loiter around or breed in some form of filth. And it's the unique way that flies are designed to eat, loiter and breed that makes them the efficient disease vectors they truly are.

Let's look closer. While loitering on infected excrement or anything that's started to decay, the fly encounters a disease-causing microorganism. This organism might attach itself to the fly's body – in which case it will survive for only a few hours – or it will be eaten and enter the fly's gut, where it persists for a number of days. Either way, this fly is now cocked and loaded to shoot off disease.

A fly has no biting gear, so it can eat things only in fluid form. When it lands on a solid food, it spits out some stomach contents and dissolves the meal into something that can be easily sucked up. But something is always left behind.

Perhaps the fly then lands directly on you – or, more indirectly, on your next meal. And perhaps the organism on board is still alive and able to infect a human host. If so, it can either be rubbed off, or excreted out of the fly's body. And the fly's characteristic way of eating helps the infective process on its way.

A note on fly physiology: because it has only a feeding tube, or proboscis, and no biting gear in its mouth, a fly can eat things only in fluid form. This means that solid or semi-solid foods have to be liquefied first. So, when finding itself on a chicken drumstick, cupcake or mound of mashed potato, the fly uses its proboscis to spit out some of its last meal – possibly, or probably, consumed on a manure pile or landfill.

This regurgitated surge contains stomach contents and digestive juices that mix with and dissolve the solid cupcake into something that can be more easily sucked up. But something is always left behind. Something from the manure pile. An infective stowaway that could make you sick.

This is not to say that flies are solely responsible for the spread of infectious disease. No, they are not that good. Often the microorganisms are too delicate to survive the flight, and in many cases transmission happens more directly through human-to-human contact or contaminated water or food. But researchers and public health pundits still agree that flies pose a significant health problem, especially in areas where refuse removal is below par and filth is more likely to accumulate. The very presence of flies can be a sign that conditions are less than hygienic. And the more flies, the less hygienic they probably are.

Think about it. More garbage and waste will attract more flies and provide more disease-causing bugs for them to pick up and carry around. This suggests that more sanitary areas will actually be home to cleaner flies. And they are. It's been established that a single fly can be home to more than 1.9 million bacteria, which is bad enough. But some scientists say that one slum-dwelling, urban fly could carry up to 33 million bacteria within its gut and half a billion more on the outside of its body. This is like an overpopulated bacterial slum living on and in a fly that itself lives in an overpopulated human slum full of people who also carry billions of bugs on and in their bodies. (Thankfully the immune system ensures that these are mostly the good sort.)

More garbage and waste will attract more flies and more disease-causing illnesses. Some scientists say that one slum-dwelling, urban fly could carry up to 33 million bacteria in its gut and half a billion more on the outside of its body.

The mind truly boggles. Considering the billions and quintillions being thrown around, it seems clear that fly infestations and fly-borne infections are more of a challenge in developing countries and communities. But developed areas and sanitised streets certainly aren't immune. Flies don't stick to one neighbourhood, they move around – within a range of up to 24 kilometres – especially if the wind picks up and gives them a push.

In any numbers, flies are always annoying. Even a single fly buzzing around a quiet kitchen is enough to spoil both the cook's mood and the broth. Unsurprising, then, that 'nuisance flies' is another semi-official title given to various groups of flies (including the housefly) that harass humans and animals through buzzing, biting and spreading disease. Nuisance flies. Filth flies. Say no more. It's all in the names.

Humans have spent hundreds or even thousands of years finding ways to kill and control flies. Which is not to say that it's worked. Despite all our time and energy, the housefly and its friends are still here and here to stay.

But flies don't just have bad PR. The facts speak for themselves. The evidence clearly shows that they really are a personal nuisance, public health hazard and potential human foe. They can't help it. It's how they are made. Maybe that's why humans have spent so much time and energy finding ways to take them apart. Which is not to say that it's worked. Despite all our time and energy, the housefly and its friends are still here and here to stay.

There was a brief period, post-World War II, when flies in homes, farms and restaurants were targeted with lashings of chlorinated hydrocarbons and DDT. A heavy-handed approach, to say the least – akin to burning down a log cabin to combat a termite problem. The toxins did put a damper on fly populations. But they also poisoned people, animals, beneficial insects and entire environments, while pushing surviving flies to develop immunity to the effects of the toxins.

The search for meaningful fly control continues. It's a testament to the insect's ability to fly in the face of our most vicious and valiant scientific eradication plans.

HOW DO HUMANS KILL FLIES?

There may be 50 ways to leave your lover, but for the purpose of this book, there are only 10 ways to kill a fly. The methods can be physical or chemical, smart or a little messy. A 2004 fly-control report by the World Health Organisation says that larger-scale, longer-term results call for preventative measures like better sanitation and improved hygiene. But, in the meantime, let's examine the 10 options available to us now, in no particular order.

1. The flyswat

Technically it's a rectangular piece of metal or plastic mesh attached to the end of a stick. More often than not it's whatever happens to be on hand – a rolled-up magazine, tea towel or (as in Obama's case) a fast, flat palm.

In some form or another, the swat is probably the oldest weapon in the fight against flies. The makeshift, make-do ones have been around forever and are pretty good at getting the job done. But the official flyswat is thought to have made its debut in 1905 in the state of Kansas, USA.

'The fly is the disseminator of the three Ds: Dirt, Diarrhoea and Disease, which often result in the three Ts: Typhoid, Tuberculosis and Toxins; and which should teach us to cultivate the three Cs: Care, Caution and Cleanliness'
— Dr Samuel Crumbine, State Board of Health, Kansas, USA, 1905

At the time, the state was suffering an influx of flies. A member of the Kansas State Board of Health, Dr Samuel Crumbine, responded with his first so-called Fly Bulletin: 'The fly is the disseminator of the three Ds: Dirt, Diarrhoea and Disease,' it said, 'which often result in the three Ts: Typhoid, Tuberculosis and Toxins; and which should teach us to cultivate the three Cs: Care, Caution and Cleanliness ...'

Crumbine's smear campaign, based out of Topeka, was as punchy as it was persuasive. '[Window] screens are cheaper than doctor's bills,' he preached, and even tried his hand at poetry: 'I never wash my feet; But every single chance I get I walk on what you eat. Buzz, buzz, busy fly.'

It was the Wild West for flies – but wilder. Especially when Crumbine started offering rewards for dead flies. A local teacher named Frank Rose heeded the call and encouraged his Boy Scout troop to help screen people's windows and make Fly Bats using offcuts of screen nailed to yardsticks. When Crumbine saw this invention, he grabbed the concept with both hands and ran with it. But he named his version the catchier Fly Swatter after hearing a fan yell, 'Swat that fly!' to a ball batted clear over the fence at a local baseball game.

Crumbine's creativity didn't stop there. He commissioned films about fly villains contaminating babies' milk. He arranged macabre `fly parades' complete with crowds of people, baskets of dead flies, giant flyswats and children dressed up as flies pushing baby-carriage coffins down the street.

In 2005 a high-tech fly-swat was invented — an electric tennis racquet-like device that fries the fly with a couple of thousand volts as it swats.

The parades were a just a phase. But the flyswat clearly was not. Since then, it's found a place in many modern homes and has even led to high-tech versions like an electric tennis racquet-like device that fries the fly with a couple of thousand volts as it swats.

Another offshoot, the fly gun, promises to squash the fly in midair by shooting out a spring-loaded, perforated plastic disk on a string.

But the basic swatter-on-a-stick variety still stands the test of time. It's thought to be a far better weapon than any flat hand or rolled-up magazine. The holes in the mesh surface allow a faster swing and fewer changes in air pressure and airflow – sensations that the fly usually senses in time to escape.

2. Sticky stuff

First there is flypaper – a roll of stickiness that's sure to ruin your appetite even if it does deal with the flies. It's usually found hanging in the centre of a room that commonly attracts flies – like a kitchen – and it's usually covered with flies in various stages of death and its preceding throes. Yes, flypaper gets the job done well.

It's designed to be suspended from the ceiling, and might contain some sugar to attract the flies. Once they are stuck, it's certain (if not immediate) death and the tape will last as long as the surface isn't covered with dust or dead flies. According to the University of Florida's Department of Entomology and Nematology, while flypaper is strung up for the smallest numbers of flies, waste management sites can collect as many as 150 flies per flypaper in a 30-minute period – thankfully most home versions don't need to work nearly as hard.

Waste management sites can collect as many as 150 flies per flypaper in a 30-minute period.

Then there are sticky boards, or glue boards, which rely on the same principle, but are often placed inside traps. This is a convenient way to keep trapped flies neatly stuck away and hidden from view. Plus, for more frugal fly killing, some boards can be washed and reused.

3. Flytraps

There are many manifestations, but the concept is consistent: irresistible bait, inescapable fate. Whether it's an old-style, glass fly bottle, a newer-fangled, plastic trap or a large, outdoor construction made of fine gauze and wood, the structure always has a very small entry hole leading into a large attractive space for breeding and feeding. That's where you place the bait, which could be anything from meat to sugar or, preferably if outdoors, decomposing kitchen waste, meat, or fish.

The trick is in the effective one-way entrance. Once the flies find their way through the hole, they can't seem to work their way out again. Some fly-bottle traps even position the hole in a narrow black metal top. Flies are positively phototaxic, or attracted to light, and therefore to any area of the trap except the dark-topped way out.

Other versions take things a step further by including a trough filled with vinegar, beer or a blend of milk, water and arsenic that the trapped flies will drown in. But, whatever form it takes, a trap is generally a very useful way to catch large numbers of flies. As long as you don't mind having to empty out those dead flies (and maggot-ridden bait) after a week or so.

4. Fly zappers

The bug zapper's earliest ancestor was probably an `electric death trap' invented in 1911. A piece of meat was used as bait to lure flies towards a light bulb surrounded by 450-volt wires.

Official people and scientists sometimes call them Devices for Electrocuting Flying Insects, or DEFLIs. But that doesn't make them any more effective. In fact, a study from the University of Notre Dame in Indiana, USA, recently showed that there was very little difference between the number of flies and mosquitoes found in homes with bug zappers and in those without.

This could be because the DEFLIs electrocute other insects more often than they do mosquitoes and flies. No matter. The devices do still have their place – mostly in hospitals, restaurant kitchens and porches belonging to eerie old guys in the movies. And they are quite cunning – the bugs are attracted to the light (through phototaxis), so they fly towards it, touch two high-voltage wires and get promptly electrocuted with a short, sharp 'zap'.

The DEFLI's earliest ancestor was probably an `electric death trap' invented by two anonymous Denver, Colorado, men and featured in a 1911 issue of *Popular Mechanics* magazine. A piece of meat as bait was used to lure flies towards a light bulb surrounded by 450-volt wires. But despite successful electrocutions and some positive press, the zap trap didn't catch on until 1934 when two different inventors in Rochester, New York, William F Folner and Harrison L Chapin, patented a fluorescent light encased in electrified wire mesh. Theirs is the invention that led to the zappers of today.

Despite this long history and their hardcore fans, the fact remains that DEFLIs don't make good solutions for fly problems. The World Health Organisation thinks they work better as part of an integrated fly-terminating programme. Most eerie guys on porches will probably agree.

5. Pheromone traps

Sex sells, but it also smells. It smells like pheromones – physiological chemicals, produced by an insect or animal to send signals to other members of its species. They are like cologne, but more effective. They might not smell as strong, but they are far more irresistible. Like cologne, pheromones are designed to sell sex by subliminally advertising an animal's sexual readiness in order to attract an appropriate mate. No one's really sure if humans produce or respond to them. But flies do. And this can be their undoing.

Sticky traps can be treated with synthetic fly sex pheromones. These natural- scented chemicals lure the fly closer in search of the mate that can be sensed but not seen. It's quite an anticlimax. The fly is stuck and remains so until it dies.

That's what happens when you add some synthetic fly sex pheromone to a sticky board or trap. An olfactory urge lures the fly closer in search of the mate that can be sensed but not seen. What follows is quite an anticlimax. The fly sticks to the board and may remain so for a day or two until it dies.

Not a great way to go. It's all morning-after, with no night-before to show for it.

Pheromone traps are very sensitive (to their targets, if not their targets' feelings). They don't work well for large numbers of flies, but are great for attracting specific breeds in low-density areas. You can seduce a fly only with a specific fly pheromone – so you know your trap won't attract and conquer every insect in the area.

The downside? They are generally single-sex operations. You can't lure male and female flies with a one-size-fits-all scent.

6. Pesticides and poisons

You can spray flies with an aerosol or pump – directly onto the fly, into the air or onto any possible landing surface. You can diffuse it in a fine mist into a warehouse or barn. You can soak it into curtains, gauze, bed nets or strips of paper. (In the old days they poured it into bunches of twigs.) You can even blast it through an area with a chemical fumigation bomb. You can use it in liquid form or as a solid dust. You can choose a quick killer or one that slays slowly over time.

In short, when it comes to flies you can have your pick of poisons. Yes, they work. But the problem with most of them is that they work on everything else, too. This can include other insects, animals, plants and any air, soil and water that might be exposed. It can also include humans who get too close.

Most common fly sprays work by inhibiting nerve signals and sending the fly into a state of paralytic contraction and fatal asphyxiation. They generally contain a strong toxin called Dichlorvos.

Since the US Environmental Protection Agency (EPA) first assessed its use in 1981, this chemical has almost been banned many times and for many reasons. It's been accused of being carcinogenic and of causing acute and chronic toxicity. It's also been linked to a possible increased risk of Attention Deficit Hyperactivity Disorder (ADHD) in children.

The other problem is that flies are speedy breeders with short lifespans. This makes them very good at developing resistance to common pesticides. What doesn't kill them makes them stronger. But it still kills or compromises the less resistant creatures in the area.

7. Toxic baits

A spoonful of sugar makes the sodium arsenite go down – "in the most delightful way". Well, sort of.

Traditionally, toxic baits mix sugar water or milk (which flies love) with strong toxins like sodium arsenite, organophosphorus or formaldehyde (which they definitely don't). Milk and sugar may be tempting, but they don't attract flies from afar – especially if there is lots of more attractive food around. It has been found that using different baits helps to lure flies over longer distances. These include fermented yeast, malt, syrup, animal protein like egg, and synthetic fly attractants or pheromones.

Traditionally, toxic baits mix sugar water or milk (which flies love) with strong toxins like sodium arsenite, organophosphorus or formaldehyde (which they definitely don't).

Toxic baits can be liquids, solids or paint-on varieties applied to fly-frequented walls, posts, windows, wires, cords or ceilings. The benefit is that they are effective for a couple of weeks. Plus they are less likely to lead to resistance. Interestingly, flies that have become immune to a particular toxin in spray-form can still be killed when it's used in bait-form.

8. Venus flytrap

When Venus shuts her trap, an airtight seal forms to keep digestive fluids in and any opportunistic bacteria out. It takes 5 to 12 days for the leaves to reopen – depending on the size of the insect.

What list of flytraps would be complete without this one? It might not kill flies in large numbers or at high speeds, but any plant that can attract, catch and digest a quick and quick-witted insect deserves mention. More than that, it deserves to be named after the Roman goddess of love. Which it is.

Just like other plants, the fly-trapping Venus gets food from the air, soil and her own photosynthetic process. But because she usually grows in acidic, nutrient-poor soil – and is found naturally in only a small boggy region of North and South Carolina in the US – she needs to supplement her diet with something. This something could be spiders, flies, caterpillars, crickets, slugs or anything else that crawls into her open-mouthed leaves, which secrete a sweet and tempting nectar to ensure that they do.

Once the something has found its way in, it invariably comes into contact with some short, sharp cilia, or hairs. These are ultra-sensitive motion-detectors. Impervious to inanimate objects, they respond immediately to any crawling or wriggling that stirs one or more of them repeatedly or in quick succession. No one is sure exactly how, but this cilial movement causes a chemical reaction that makes the plant tissue relax and the two lobes swing towards one another. This takes about a second. But there has to be movement. That's why delivering a self-swatted fly to Venus isn't enough – you have to move it around within the trap before she accepts the sacrifice and eats.

This goddess also knows exactly what she wants to eat and won't be satisfied with anything else. Flies fit the bill perfectly because of their size and composition. That's why, when the leaves swing closed they remain slightly open for a few seconds to allow smaller insects to escape – they are just not worth the effort. Also, if an inedible object happens to fall in and trip the trap, the leaves will open after about 12 hours so that the leaf or stone can be `spat' out.

If and when she gets what she ordered, Venus shuts her trap tight. An airtight seal forms around the meal to keep the digestive fluids in and any opportunistic bacteria out. It takes five to 12 days for the leaves to reopen – depending on the size of the insect – but when Venus is done digesting, nothing remains except perhaps a tough insect exoskeleton that will be washed or blown away.

Clever, carnivorous Venus. She might be endangered in the wild, but – like the flies she hunts and eats – she has also evolved to survive. Now this plant has become a collectors' choice and a source of sport. She even has humans catching and hand-feeding her flies in their homes. Not too demanding. Two a month is generally enough.

9. Fly predators

For $20 to $30 you can buy one unit of parasitic wasps online. That's about 10,000 fly pupae infected with wasps and packed in a paper bag full of sawdust. Plus they will ship anywhere. Sounds like a bargain. If you know what to do with them.

This is called biocontrol – the agricultural management of one pest (like flies) using another pest (like wasps). It's a smart system because it exploits the natural hunter-prey relationship. When flies are the proposed prey, hunters of choice can include several predatory beetles and mites, or else the tiny parasitic wasps that love to take over fly pupae.

It's called biocontrol – the agricultural management of one pest (like flies) using another pest (like parasitic, pupae-infesting wasps).

Many insectaries specialise in breeding and selling these wasps. And many farmers buy them because they make a great fly-control workforce. Parasitic wasps will work against the housefly, lesser housefly, biting stable fly, blowfly and bottle fly. They also reduce

Parasitic wasps are biologically drawn to fly pupae and larvae about to pupate. They can travel 30 to 50 metres to seek out and infect a host, even at a depth of up to 20 centimetres in manure.

or eliminate the need for unnatural insecticides – particularly useful on farms where humans, animals and crops risk toxic exposure.

The safety features continue. These wasps are host-specific, meaning any exposed humans, animals and crops are perfectly safe. Also, they want fly pupae and not much else – they are biologically drawn to the pupae, as well as to larvae that are about to pupate. In fact they can travel 30 to 50 metres to seek out and infect a host, even at a depth of up to 20 centimetres in manure (the birth and growth place of many flies in farm environments).

When a wasp finds a pupa, it breaks open the shell and lays an egg inside. The pupa dies on exposure to air, and when the wasp egg hatches, the pupal juices and remains provide a convenient source of food. Adult wasps also feed on fly pupae fluid – they eat twice during their 16 to 28-day adulthood and will reproduce as soon as they leave the puparium, laying six to 350 eggs a day, which yield more natural-born killers to join the fray.

This safe, sustainable and self-renewing workforce is similar to those produced by Integrated Pest Management (IPM) companies like Oxitec. Like the parasitic wasp producers, they breed insects to manage pests. But, in this case, they breed the pests themselves – more specifically, pest insects that carry disease or damage crops, such as mosquitoes and fruit flies, respectively. During the breeding process, fancy, biotechnological interventions produce sterile males that are released into the environment to mate fruitlessly with wild females and keep populations in check. It's a highly targeted form of biocontrol that's adding its clout to the pesticide fight.

And it's a fight that's ongoing. The biocontrol industry as been growing since the 1950s when the first murmurings about long-term pesticide dangers were heard. The US Agricultural Research Service estimates that since 1953 this approach has saved more than $2 billion in pesticides. That said, according to Oxitec, despite the use of around $8 billion of pesticides a year, insects still claim at least 20 to 40 percent of the agriculturally grown food. Clearly, there is still an important place for pest management using pests.For parasitic wasps that place is within the fly pupae they know and love.

Despite the use of around $8 billion of pesticides a year, insects still claim at least 20 to 40 percent of the agriculturally grown food.

10. The Obama method

You don't need to be the President to successfully swat a fly. But being a scientist might give you an edge. Just ask fly bioengineer and professor at the California Institute of Technology, Michael Dickinson – although, after 20 years spent studying fly aerodynamics, the prof is probably quite tired of being asked how best to squash the subjects he studies so hard.

In 2008 Dickinson (Flyman to his friends and according to his official university email address) used high-speed digital videos of fruit flies to assess their swatter-dodging ability. His research, published in the journal Current Biology, showed how this escape reflex is hardwired into the fly brain and allows it to react within 100 thousandths of a second.

First the fly brain calculates the location of the incoming swatter and – depending on its angle of approach – immediately positions its legs, wings and centre of mass for an optimal leap out of the way. Fortunately (or unfortunately for the swat wielder) the fly has a near 360-degree field of view that makes sneaking up difficult (although not impossible).

If the threat comes from up ahead, the fly's legs and weight are arranged to push off backwards – vice versa if it approaches from behind. A swat from the side leads the fly to lean and then jump in the opposite direction. 'The fly somehow knows whether it needs to make large or small changes to reach the correct preflight posture,' says Dickinson. And the result is a super-speedy getaway from spider, bird, lizard or striking human hand.

Nevertheless, on-target swatting is as simple as anticipating the very speed that makes the fly likely to evade your swat in the first place. Dickinson explains that the aim is to aim a little ahead of the fly's starting position. In other words, go for the direction you know the fly will leap to avoid your swing.

Flyman also has the following tips for more effective swatting:

- **Think before you swing.** Before swatting, approach and position the swatter slowly. Then swing fast.
- **Go back to front.** The fly can see almost full-circle around itself. The operative word is `almost'. Visibility isn't 100 percent in the rear, so it's always better to approach from behind.
- **Use a matching swatter.** A neutral-coloured flyswat (as opposed to a dark or bright one) will blend in with the background.
- **Don't swat on the move.** To improve your chances, take your aim and make your move when the fly is stationary – when in flight it can change course in just 30-thousandths of a second.

Despite these swatting tips, Dickinson's work is not really about killing flies. Rather it's about what we can learn from the insect's unique abilities (read more about his robotic flies and their aerodynamic lessons for man in Chapter 6). One of these most impressive abilities is an incredible capacity to survive. Which brings us once again to the reason humans have to try so hard to kill flies in the first place.

In an attempt to understand their drive to survive, Professor Emeritus Andrew Beckenbach from Simon Fraser University in Canada has used fly DNA analysis to paint a picture of the species' evolutionary history. It's a panoramic picture that spans 250 million years, and is part of an even broader effort to understand the evolutionary tree of which we are all a part. One thing is certain: flies constitute an important branch of this tree. According to Beckenbach they make up 7.5 percent of all species known to man.

> Flies seem to defy mass extinctions. The most recent one swatted dinosaurs from the Earth around 65 million years ago. But flies thrived.

Beckenbach's fly family portrait was published in the journal Proceedings of the National Academy of Sciences (PNAS) in March 2011. It shows that there have been at least three episodes of fly-adaptive radiation, or adaption of one ancestor species into a number of new distinct species. The most recent radiation started about 65 million years ago and ended (or rather continues) in `modern' species like the housefly and fruit fly.

More interesting is the fact that flies seem to defy mass extinctions – like the last one, which swatted the dinosaurs from the Earth around 65 million years ago. Beckenbach notes that flies didn't just survive this large-scale, multi-species destruction. On the contrary -- at the time, they thrived.

Clearly, flies predate humans and survived the dinosaurs. They can outfly, outbreed and outlast our best brains and most brilliant poisons and traps. They reproduce in quintillions, carry bacteria by the billions and take human lives by the millions upon millions, just by doing what they do.

They defy mass extinctions and continuously deny scientists, presidents and secretaries of public health the pleasure of their permanent demise. Despite our greatest efforts, there are always more flies. We treat them like enemies, but they are part of a perfectly balanced system of mutual destruction and bilateral need. Although we kill them, they need us (and our waste) to survive. It might be that our survival depends on them. Perhaps we should start seeing them as friends.

CHAPTER 3

FLY AS FRIEND

IF THE FLY WERE a superhero, it would be the Incredible Hulk. The hero we love, hate and fear simultaneously. Why? Because he is a combination of power and danger in one potent package. It doesn't take much. At the slightest provocation, the Hulk's strength slides quickly into destruction. That's probably why most of us would be happy to count him as a friend, even as we tut and shake our heads at his tendency to roar, triple in size and then run around destroying things in a pair of torn shorts.

The same goes for the fly. As evidenced in Chapter 2, it makes a very good human enemy. But only if we focus on its antisocial habits as opposed to its inherent strengths.

There are more than 120,000 species of flies, which range in size from a fraction of an inch to well over three inches.

Clearly, the fly is both good guy and bad guy combined. It comes in more than 120,000 species that range in size from a fraction of an inch to well over three inches. One thing they all have in common is their two wings – other insect species all have four. Another common talent is the ability to mate and reproduce efficiently and ultra-fast – a feature that, in agricultural and social circles at least, might brand the fly as a pest. A pesky picnic-spoiler and crop-wrecker at best.

But this finely tuned life cycle might also brand the fly as our friend. It's definitely something of a strength. It could even be a superpower.

THE FLY: A LIFE STORY

It's a story in four parts: 1) egg, 2) larva or maggot, 3) pupa, and 4) adult fly. From start to finish, the whole thing usually takes between one and three weeks, although in cooler, less fly-friendly conditions, it can stretch out to two or three months. Where does it start? That all depends on your own, personal answer to the eternal question: Which comes first, the chicken (or the fly) or the egg? But let's sidestep the causality dilemma for now. It doesn't matter anyway. What does matter is that flies lay eggs and eggs lead to more flies. Let's begin (for no particular reason) with the egg.

Part 1: Egg

Over three to four days, a female housefly can lay up to 800 small, white eggs of just over one millimetre in length. She lays them in batches of 75 to 150 at a time. A larger female will produce more eggs, as will one that does her oviposition (or egg laying) at optimal humidity and temperatures of 25° to 30°C.

In some species the female actually skips the laying and the larvae hatch from the eggs while they are still in her body. This is called ovoviviparity. Or saving time.

The egg stage is a short one. Hatching usually occurs immediately or within a few hours. In some species the female actually skips the laying and the larvae hatch from the eggs while they are still in her body. This is called ovoviviparity – or saving time. But, whether a fly is oviparous (egg-laying) or ovoviviparous (egg-retaining), when it comes to hatching, it's all about location, location, location.

Females do their laying within or as close as possible to a food source for the hatchling larvae. Plus the eggs need to remain moist or they won't hatch. That's why prime blow fly and flesh fly breeding sites include juicy meat or carrion. According to research quoted in the Encyclopedia of Entomology, houseflies prefer (in descending order) horse manure, human excrement, cow manure, rotting vegetables and kitchen waste.

Part 2: Larva or maggot

This part of the story sees our hero make its first transformation, from egg to maggot. Most species of fly larvae are slim, white squirming things without legs, no real eyes and very little distinction between the head and every other body part – although a mouth gives some definition to one end. This is quite obviously the aesthetic low point in a generally aesthetically challenged existence. Flies may not be lookers at any point. But the larval stage is like their teenagehood – a gangly, interim phase where eating and growing take precedence over just about everything else.

Flies may not be lookers at any point. But the larval stage is like their teenagehood – a gangly, interim phase where eating and growing take precedence over just about everything else.

This is why larvae are such featureless creatures. They are perfectly adapted to burrowing through the moist and nutritious mess in which they find themselves, eating and growing with abandon. If the breeding material is wet, the larvae will stay on the surface where they can access fresh air and oxygen. If it's drier, they will hunker down several centimetres deep to find moisture and food. But, regardless of the medium, their bodies are designed for writhing and dining.

Between a mouth hole for incoming food and an anus for outgoing waste, they consist of not much more than a muscular tube around an intestine. Some species have added features like two big salivary glands. But they all have spiracles or breathing holes – and mostly around the anus, in the rear, which means they really never have to stop eating. Even to breathe.

But temperature (as opposed to time) is of the essence during the three larval instars, or stages of development. In their first instar, larvae are two millimetres in length. They can grow to 20 millimetres in four to 13 days, moulting twice and moving through their second and third instars along the way. Larval survival is greatest at 17° to 32°C. Once again, lowertemperatures can slow their development, which might take more than twice the time at 12° to 17°C.

But, when it comes to survival, fly larvae would be on the back foot, if they had feet. Unfortunately for the larvae – but fortunately for the birds, fish, lizards and many other animals that like to eat them – these squirmy, wormy things make a great source of both calories

Research has shown that larvae are packed with a hefty 55 percent protein. So it's no wonder they have such a hard time avoiding being eaten.

and protein. In fact, research has shown that they are packed with a hefty 55 percent protein. So it's no wonder they have such a hard time not being eaten. It's no wonder they have to try so hard to escape being snacked on and to survive.

One key larval escape trick is to `see' with their whole bodies. Like having eyes in the back of their heads, and everywhere else too. Larvae do have rudimentary, eye-type structures called Bolwig's organs, which can perceive objects and movement right in front of them. Well, sort of. But this doesn't really help when a larva is burrowing Bolwig's organ-first into a pile of putrefying mush.

What does help is that larvae hate light. According to research by the University of California published in the journal Nature in December 2010, larvae like those of the fruit fly are covered with light-sensing neurons that help them stay out of trouble even when their Bolwig's organs have been removed. This full-body sight-suit helps the larvae squirm away from desiccating sunlight and exposure to predators. Housefly larvae can do it too. In fact, while a younger housefly larva is repelled by light to dig deeper (and safer) into the breeding matter, an older one will grow into a sudden attraction to light that draws it towards the brighter, drier surface around the instar. This makes perfect sense considering what comes next.

When it's finally reached full size and amassed the essential nutrients needed for the next developmental step, the maggot is ready to move on. It will writhe its way under objects or across distances of more than 15 metres to find just the right cool, dark, dry place for pupation. Which brings us to our hero's final transformation.

Part 3: Pupa

It all happens in the puparium – a kind of capsule that forms around the larva that's ready to pupate. It can take many shapes and, depending on the species, can be made of anything from the larva's own outer chitin layer to a cocoon of silk. This is where the transmutation into adult fly takes place. It's like a changing room cubicle. Or, in the case of a superhero, the closest phone booth for a change on the quick.

It usually takes two to 10 days for the larva-to-fly transformation to occur – during which time the skin-derived pupal case can also change colour from yellow to red to brown to black. When it's ready, the newly formed fly breaks out of the case using a convenient sac on its head called the ptilinum. By alternately expanding and contracting the sac it hammers right through the wall and into the blue yonder beyond. Our hero is officially an adult fly and ready to take flight. Its body dries and hardens as it spreads its wings.

Part 4: Adult fly

A day in the life of an adult fly is a very, very long time. After all the effort of eating, expanding and metamorphosing, a fully grown housefly usually lives for only 15 to 25 days. So every day really does count. It counts for the equivalent of five years of human life in fact – unless the fly is one of the luckier ones that manage to live for up to two months.

In general, fly lifespan is directly proportional to the presence of moisture, ideal temperatures and food – especially the right kind of food, like sugar. Flies need to feed at least two or three times a day and get a drink of water even more urgently and often. Without enough food and fluids, it's all over in two or three days.

Flies need to feed at least twice a day and get a drink of water even more urgently and often. Without enough food and fluids, it's all over in two or three days.

What do they like to drink? Just about anything wet – and they will do anything to get it. Hence their tendency to end up floating in any cup of tea left unattended on a desk. What do they like to eat? As much as possible. Some firm favourites are milk, syrup, sugar, blood and meat broth. But in natural conditions flies will seek out a highly diverse menu, including most human and animal food, garbage, excreta and even sweat.

It takes four to five days for adult flies to reach reproductive maturity. But that doesn't mean they dive straight into the reproductively mature deed. Once again, food is a key factor. Evidently, the way to a fly's heart (or at least to its genitals) is through its stomach. If the right fly-friendly food is available, copulation will commence and the whole thing takes anything from two to 15 minutes. Quick it is, but simple it isn't.

Research has shown that the male housefly is like an erotic elastic band, both inside and out. Before mating, an intricate muscular system twists his abdomen a full 360° and internally wraps the reproductive organs around his gut.

Fly sex is an epic act of airborne and sometimes acrobatic proportions. Firstly, female fly genitalia are naturally rotated into various alignments that differ from those of other insects. Secondly, research published in New Scientist (1990) has shown that the male housefly in particular is something of an erotic elastic band, both inside and out. Before mating, an intricate muscular system twists his abdomen a full 360°. This external torsion causes an internal ripple effect that wraps the reproductive organs around is gut. It's a timely contortion that allows the right male and female bits to meet in more conformations than most other insects could even imagine. But this Kama Sutra of twisted intertwining is not unique to the housefly. In fact, of all 120,000 or so species of fly, almost every male can contort through anything from 180° to 360°. As a result, flies can mate quickly and efficiently, some on a hard surface, some in the air – with the male fly on top facing forward, backward, up or down. All it takes is a twist in the right direction.

But that's not all. The fly's sexual bag of tricks can also include lust-fanning pheromones – some species spread the scented substances over their wings and flap them in a mate's direction. And then there are the fruit fly's penile spines or anatomical Velcro. Seriously. That's even what the entomologists are calling them.

In 2009, Michal Polak and Arash Rashed, two researchers from the University of Cincinnati, were investigating the bristles or spines that surround the fruit fly genital zone – by 'investigating' we mean they shaved them off with a laser. The results were good for science, but bad for fly sex lives. Conclusions published in the journal of The Royal Society of Biological Sciences, Proceedings B (January 2010) showed that without these specialised spines, the male's chances of mating successfully dropped to a mere 20 percent – despite the fact that he courted, mounted and positioned himself on the female just right.

Usually, when the spines and an available female are firmly in place, a male fruit fly is just about certain to score. These spiky structures clearly help the male get a better grip on his mate – in the correct position, and for long enough to inject sperm. They have also been found to move rhythmically over each other to help secure the genital connection even further. The Velcro stays. Fruit fly bikini waxes will never catch on.

When they are not mating, laying eggs or eating, adult flies are quite serious about resting. Especially at night. They are also quite serious about their resting places. They will stop only in spots that are nicely sheltered and close to food and breeding grounds. Indoors, they like ceilings and other overhead structures like beams and wires. Outdoors, they prefer trees, shrubs, grasses, electric wires, fences, clotheslines, latrines or garbage bins – usually elevated, but rarely more than five metres high (which is still enough to keep us looking up to them).

When the male fly's Velcro or genital spines were shaved off with a laser, his chances of mating successfully dropped to a mere 20 percent.

About 20 days after the fly couple copulates, a new generation is already into the egg-stage of the cycle. Clearly, flies are excellent breeders. At cooler temperatures, they will produce 10 to 12 generations a year – in subtropical and tropical climates this can climb to as many as 20. In fact, good breeding is one of the superpowered strengths that could help flies save the world. As we will soon see.

THE FLY: A FAMILY STORY

True flies belong to the order *Diptera*, which means 'two wings'. They may share certain traits – like two-wingedness and abdominal twisting – but the hundreds of thousands of species also each have their own distinct talents and features. If we really want to make friends with flies, we need to know which ones are good at what. It's a giant family tree. But let's explore a few major branches.

Flies can be classified according to 1) whether or not they like to be indoors, and 2) whether or not they like to bite. That's very simply put. In scientific terms, it's way more complicated. Of the most common flies, it's clear that some like to breed and develop indoors, while others complete their life cycle outside and come inside only at certain times, in search of shelter. It's also clear that, while some flies have only harmless suction gear for sipping up liquids, others have biting gear and the will to use it.

Let's briefly meet and greet some of the fly species you're likely to encounter later in this book. And let's start with the most famous house-dwelling, non-biting fly of them all. The common housefly, *Musca domestica*.

The housefly

The housefly is as common as dirt, and it loves dirt – especially garbage, excrement, rotting food and decaying meat or flesh.

Found in houses and just about everywhere else, this is the most omnipresent and therefore one of the peskiest flies around. It's as common as dirt, and it loves dirt – especially garbage, excrement, rotting food and decaying meat or flesh. It likes to lay its eggs in all of the above places. These then hatch into larvae that have a hook-like, sucking mouthpart, or proboscis, for feeding on the moist organic matter all around them. They use this matter to fuel significant growth into bigger, sausage-shaped larvae stuffed with protein, fat and hard-won nutrients.

Research has shown that housefly larvae are made up of about 55 percent protein – one South Korean study even estimates that they contain up to 64 percent protein and 24 percent fat. Either way, these larvae have been found to be a protein source that's equal to other animal protein, such as meat and fish. Nutritionally, they surpass another well-known protein source, soybean meal.

> Research has shown that housefly larvae are made up of about 55% protein. Peanuts are less than half as rich with a protein content of just 25%.

This doesn't mean we should be popping housefly maggots like peanuts – which, incidentally, according to the American Peanut Council, are less than half as protein-rich at 25 percent. But it does mean that these larvae might have an indirect role to play in human nutrition. More on that later.

The adult housefly also has a sucking proboscis and doesn't bite. It can only ingest fluids and prefers sugar and dirt to blood (which it eats by means of the characteristic spit-up-slurp-down process). Physically and behaviourally, this is the definitive fly. The typical, typecast one seen in many kids' cartoons and Renaissance trompe l'oeil paintings. It is six to seven millimetres long, hairy and triangular in shape. It has four black stripes on its thorax and a habit of rubbing its front legs together. It also has big reddish eyes – the male's almost touch, while the female's are more widely spaced. The female is also usually bigger (in case you can't get a close enough look at the eyes).

The blowfly

Like the housefly, the blunt-mouthed blowfly also likes to infest houses and doesn't bite. That said, it does have a taste for non-human flesh – its eggs are usually laid in animal carcasses, rotting meat or rubbish containing meat scraps, all of which make ideal food sources for the carrion-loving larvae that will hatch.

In urban areas, the blowfly can be even more abundant than the ever-abundant housefly. But, in the fly kingdom, the blowfly is queen.

The beauty queen, that is. Prettier than most, she has a characteristic shiny, metallic body in copper, green, blue or black. This has spawned the nickname `bluebottle' or `greenbottle'. That, or Miss Diptera. The choice is yours.

The black soldier fly

Is it a lieutenant? No. Is it a corporal? No. Is it a soldier? Yes. But it's also a fly – not that you'd think so by looking at it.

The black soldier fly looks more like a wasp. It even has two small transparent bits near the second abdominal segment that give the illusion of a narrow wasp waist.

Anatomically the black soldier fly looks more like a wasp. More specifically, the organ pipe mud dauber wasp, which also has long, forward-projecting antennae and pale, yellowish forelegs. To complete the picture, this fly has two small transparent bits near the second abdominal segment that give the illusion of a narrow wasp waist. Like those high-fashion frocks with slimming panels on the hips.

But it's more than just a striking silhouette. This fly is special because only its larvae need to feed. The adult fly has no biting apparatus and doesn't eat waste of any sort – that's why this species is not associated with pestering people, transmitting disease or doing much at all. The adult black soldier is a feeble flier that usually spends its time taking it easy in and around farm areas. Its name is clearly inspired by form and not function.

But the larval phase is a lot more interesting and industrious. Black soldier larvae eat and grow with military efficiency. They are detritivores – they feed on detritus or decaying waste – and they have big, strong, chewing gear for shredding and churning up decomposing organic matter, such as manure or compost heaps. And they make useful additions to both, mostly because they digest the material before it has time to decompose. The result? Less odour, less waste, and a less attractive environment for more pesky kinds of flies, because the black soldier larvae blend the detritus into a more liquid form, making it a less inviting place for egg laying and larval development.

That's why some clever people have put black soldier larvae to work in waste management and pest control – at one point they were even called privy flies for their ability to help keep less-than-welcome houseflies out of less-than-sanitary outhouses. Plus, because these larvae can process manure into a 42 percent protein, 35 percent fat substance that's rich in nutrients like calcium, they have also found a place in pet and livestock feed. It's called bioconversion. More on that in Chapter 10.

Black soldier fly larvae have big, strong, chewing gear for shredding and churning up decomposing organic matter, such as manure or compost heaps – both of which they can help to deodorise and digest.

The fruit fly

It's a yellow-brown fly with fetching red eyes. Scientists call it by its Latin name, *Drosophila*. They spend a lot of time cursing it, writing about it and shouting it from the rooftops. In fact, there is a whole family of *Drosophilidae* flies. But researchers really have eyes only for the common fruit fly, vinegar fly or *Drosophila melanogaster*. That's Greek for `dark-bellied dew lover'. How romantic. Especially for a scientist.

But the fruit fly is easy to fall for – and not just because the white-coat brigade doesn't get out much. In addition to being a rather run-of-the-mill, non-biting house-infester that likes drains, sewers and rotting or overripe fruits, vegetables and plants, *Drosophila* is an academic dream. It's quick to breed, easy to rear, and capable of laying many, many eggs. It also exhibits sexual dimorphism, which means it's easy to tell who's who in the lab. Females are a couple of centimetres longer than the males, who also have a distinct black patch on their abdomens – as well as the spiky sexual Velcro around their genitals described earlier.

It's a genetic match made in heaven. Around 75 percent of known human disease genes have an equivalent in the fruit fly genome.

All in all, *Drosophila* is one of the most often-studied organisms in genetics, physiology and evolutionary biology. It's already being used as a genetic model for research into ageing, immunity, diabetes, cancer and neurodegenerative conditions like Parkinson's disease, Huntington's disease, and Alzheimer's. This is because it's a genetic match made in heaven for humans – around 75 percent of known human disease genes have an equivalent in the *Drosophila* genome. In fact, the University of California's Division of Biological Sciences now runs an online database for shared human and fruit fly disease genes. It's called Homophila. A sharing of names, too.

The biting flies

Non-biters are enough of a pain. They arrive uninvited and make themselves at home in our homes. They also bring along baggage like picked-up filth and infectious organisms. But at least houseflies, blowflies and fruit flies don't have the capacity to stalk living creatures by sensing exhaled carbon dioxide and moisture, sweat, dark colours, warmth and movement. And at least they, when found, don't have sharp mouthparts that can be used to break through skin and inject anticoagulant-containing saliva that keeps blood flowing. This they leave to the biters like horseflies, sandflies, stable flies and midges. And they are the real pains.

Biting flies are responsible for spreading certain dangerous infections to large numbers of people. Sandflies can spread sandfly fever and disfiguring leishmaniasis. One type of biting deer fly can carry tularaemia or rabbit fever. Horseflies can transmit various human and animal blood-borne infections, including filarial worms and even anthrax in cattle. Then there are tiny biting midges or gnats that can carry a range of diseases (including the disturbing-sounding blue tongue virus that infects cattle), and will suck the blood of humans or other insects like mosquitoes.

To add allergy to injury, the saliva of flies like the horse, black and stable fly can also trigger potentially fatal reactions in sensitive individuals.

The horsefly, specifically, is a fast, furious and infamous biter. At an inch or more in length, it's also one of the largest flies around. It likes to feed on the blood of cattle and other animals. Or at least the female does; the male horsefly only has the mouthparts for pollen or nectar. There are over 4,000 species of horsefly, which can be anything from black to pale brown with shiny green eyes (these are known as greenheads). They can have a short, sharp proboscis that cuts flesh like a knife, or a longer, needle-like one that works much like a mosquito's.

Biting flies stalk living creatures by sensing exhaled carbon dioxide and moisture, sweat, dark colours, warmth and movement.

Wild horses couldn't drag Mick Jagger away from the person he was singing about. But wild horseflies might manage. Their bite is fast and the reaction often an extreme combination of pain, itching and swelling. Blood loss can also be significant in animals – a US Department of Agriculture Bulletin has estimated that 20 to 30 horse-flies could consume 20 teaspoons of blood in six hours, or almost a litre in ten days. When horseflies descend in swarms, some animals can lose up to 300 ml of blood in a day, which is enough to weaken or even kill them.

Like deer flies, horsefly larvae usually live in moist earth or ponds. The eggs are laid on stones or plants nearby and the hatchling larvae fall in and feed on snails, earthworms and other insects while they grow. Because they often wait for spring to pupate and overwinter as larvae, the horsefly life cycle usually takes a whole year – sometimes two. Adults also live an impressive 30 to 60 days. In fly terms, that's practically immortal.

So-called black flies, too, have a taste for blood. A taste that can see them flying distances up to 16 kilometres to find it. They don't transmit disease, but when numbers rise, their combined bites can be enough to kill both cattle and humans. Stable flies will also go the distance for a drink. Besides its pointy, blood-sucking proboscis that can stab right through clothing, this fly looks a lot like the housefly – which might explain why it's also called the biting housefly. In addition to livestock, horses and humans, dogs in outdoor kennels often suffer bad stable fly bites – particularly on their legs and ear tips. The biting housefly is in the doghouse.

It's okay to poke fun at the stable fly. But not at the tsetse fly. There is nothing funny about an insect whose bite can lead from headache, fever, swelling and joint pain into a slow slide towards sleep, madness, coma and death. Actually this sleeping sickness or trypanasomiasis is caused by the trypanosome protozoa, which is transmitted by the tsetse fly to humans and animals in 36 African countries.

Tsetse fly bites – and the trypanosome protozoa they carry – cause sleeping sickness. A slow slide from headache, fever, swelling and joint pain towards sleep, madness, coma and death.

Although control is better than ever before, it still kills thousands of people every year. According to the World Health Organisation, the estimated number of cases is around 30,000, although in 2009 only 9,878 cases were reported, the first time in 50 years that the official number dipped below 10,000. But, of the 30-something species of tsetses (depending on the classification system you use), only six are possible carriers of the two kinds of trypanosomes that cause either acute or chronic sleeping sickness – both of which are fatal if left untreated.

It's not a scary-looking fly. In fact, it's scary how ordinary it seems. It's housefly-sized and yellowish brown, with two wings and large, wide eyes. But there are two anatomical warning signs that distinguish the tsetse from its non-killing cousins. Firstly, while resting, it folds its wings one on top of the other to look like a pair of closed scissors. Secondly, a long, forward-reaching proboscis is attached to the bottom of its head by a distinct bulb. It looks like a silver spoon in the mouth. This is quite appropriate, considering that tsetse fly young are probably the most mollycoddled of all flies. The entire lifestyle and parent-larva relationship is more than a little dysfunctional. Not least of which because the female tsetse produces just one egg at a time that hatches inside its uterus and emerges only as a third-phase larva to burrow into the ground and pupate. This it continues to do every nine days or so for the rest of its adult life.

Compared with other larvae which have to fend for themselves, the tsetse fly larva is spoilt. It happily sponges off its mother from day one – after hatching within the protective confines of its body, it feeds on a milky substance secreted by a uterine gland and hordes all the nutrition required for both larval development and pupation into an adult. Therefore, the female has to provide enough energy for both itself and the overindulged only child until it reaches adulthood. No tough love in the tsetse fly family.

Tsetse flies are the most mollycoddled of all flies. The female produces one egg at a time that hatches within its body and feeds on a milky uterine secretion. This is why it has to eat (and bite) for two.

This is called K-selection, a form of adaptation to a usually stable environment that includes fewer offspring and attentive parental care until maturity. It's highly unusual for insects. In fact, it's more common in large organisms like elephants, whales, tigers, humans, trees and some smaller rodents. The result is that the overtaxed tsetse female has to eat for two. This it does with gusto. Like her male counterpart, she feeds on blood – mostly from animals and only accidentally from humans – and is drawn to carbon dioxide, large moving things (like animals), dark colours (like animal hides) and, for some reason, things that are strikingly blue (like many tsetse fly traps that exploit this fatal attraction).

For some reason, tsetse flies are drawn to things that are strikingly blue. Many tsetse fly traps are blue to exploit this fatal attraction.

For us, preventing tsetse fly bites involves scanning for the scissor-winged, silver-spooned flies and avoiding dusty and brushy areas – especially in the hottest part of the day when tsetses rest, but bite if disturbed. It also includes covering up with insect repellent, protective clothing and bed nets. But nothing too bright-coloured or too dark, which might prove to be more attractive than protective. Similarly, jeans, blue T-shirts or bedsheets are clearly potentially fatal faux pas.

Maybe the tsetse fly is not a friend to humans. But it still belongs in this chapter. Even though it transmits sleeping sickness, it can also help us to control the disease. How? Through the Sterile Insect Technique (SIT) – the breeding and releasing of irradiated, sterile tsetse males into high-risk areas to curb populations.

More about this technique and the flies that further it in later chapters. In the meantime, here's Chapter 4: a roundup of even more cool tricks and fancy features that make good fly-friend material.

CHAPTER 4

SEVEN WONDERS OF THE FLY

AND NOW FOR SOMETHING completely different. The seven wonders of the fly. A random roundup of fly facts and features that don't seem to fit anywhere else in this book.

Each fact is something completely different. A reason to wonder even more at this insect's inherent abilities and applications in various fields. At the very least, each is also a good `Did-you-know?' dinner party conversation titbit. Or else just a good reason to say Wow!

1. Their eyes

Many insects have complex and compound eyes. But even the crudest human eyes can see that the fly's are among the most complex and compound of them all. They are made up of around 4,000 individual optical units apiece. Each unit detects light, has its own lens and is hexagonal, which means it can be packed tightly against the others and avoid gaps in a way that no other shape can.

Although each lens detects light and generates an image of its own, this doesn't mean the fly spies the world in chopped-up fragments. A network of nerves manages the signals generated, producing a single image in wider-than-wide-angle vision. Impressive to us, this is nothing new to flies. Their visual set-up is as ancient as they are. And it's still better than our newer-fangled versions.

The fly eye can perceive light vibrations at a rate of 330 times a second. It can also detect ultraviolet frequencies invisible to humans – which is why flies can find food and dodge swats in the dark.

The fly eye can perceive light vibrations at a rate of 330 times a second. It can also detect ultraviolet frequencies invisible to humans. That's one of the reasons the fly is so good at scouting out danger and dodging our attacks. What chance do we have? Fly sight is about six times more sensitive than ours.

Even Bette Davis' eyes had nothing on the fly's. Although Bette did have eyelids – the fly doesn't and therefore has to rub its eyes with its feet to keep them clean. The eye of a horsefly can reflect light to form a rainbow. And the housefly's wraparound, almost full-circle model has inspired researchers from École Polytechnique Fédérale de Lausanne in Switzerland to invent a neat little camera that can photograph and film in a full 360°.

Like the housefly eye that inspired it, the little convex camera takes in images from all directions and then reconstructs them in 3D. As creatures who have a paltry visual field of 120° (most of which is peripheral vision and ignored anyway), we humans can't possibly comprehend what it means to see so many things from so many angles simultaneously. But flies can. And so might the cars and robots that one day might have proximity sensors that utilise this 360°, fly-eye-inspired camera. The camera could also add new dimensions to media experiences like online gaming, as well as enabling viewing concerts or sporting events from any location – on the field or stage, in the stands, from above, or from any other fly's-eye view possible.

2. Their hairs

Flies are like small, hairy beasts. Their bodies are literally covered with hairs, and not just to make them look more unpleasant than they already do. These hairs or bristles earn their keep. They are hardworking, sensory structures that help the fly stay in touch with its environment.

> Chemosensory hairs on the fly's feet allow a potential food source to be tasted while walking across it.

They can be mechanosensory for movement and pressure, or chemosensory for taste and smell. It depends where they are located. Body hairs bend when touched, so are used by the fly both to smell and feel the things around them. Antennae also make useful additional sniffing gear. Naturally, the hairs on the mouthparts are used for tasting. Not so naturally, so are those on the feet. It's a two-step taste test: first the fly samples a potential food source while walking across it. Then, if it likes what the foot hairs have to say, it brings in the hairy mouthparts to taste the substance again.

3. Their wings

Two wings good, four wings bad. Certainly if you're a fly. In a world of four-winged insects, true flies are defined by their single pair. Although that is not strictly true – in reality, flies do have four wings. The hind two just don't do much to keep the insect airborne, meaning they are not technically wings and don't add to the final count.

In reality, flies do have four wings. But the hind two don't do much to keep the insect airborne, meaning they are not technically wings and don't add to the final count.

While the fly's front two membranous wings are responsible for flight, the rear two are reduced in size and function to a supporting role. They are called halteres – one millimetres long, lollipop-shaped structures that are thought to have evolved (or devolved) from a proper pair of hind wings that ancestral flies must have had. They do beat – at the same speed as their front counterparts in fact – but they do so only to ensure better balance and navigation. They are not much more than rudders or gyroscopes, bringing up the rear. But without them, the fly might not manage to fly straight, or at all.

Human muscle fibres can contract about 10 or 11 times a second. At most. Fly wings have to flap 200 times a second just to stay airborne. At full steam, this can increase to around 345 flaps every second. But at any speed, fly wings in flight result in an impressive flurry of activity and agility that allows for hovering, full-circle turning and rapid changes of direction as well as flying forward, backward and even upside down. Musical types might be interested to know that this flapping flurry results in a characteristic hum that falls in the middle octave key of F minor.

4. Their speed

In 1927, after much observation on a mountain slope in New Mexico, at a height of some 12,000 feet, American entomologist Charles Townsend stated that deer botflies could fly faster than any other insect, at speeds of up to 1,287 kilometres per hour. That's faster than the speed of sound. It's also highly unlikely.

The fastest fly is thought to be the male horsefly, which has been found capable of catching a plastic pellet fired from an air rifle at 145 kilometres per hour or more.

Even so, Townsend's allegedly record-breaking deer bots made it into *The New York Times*, the Journal of the New York Entomological Society and the *Guinness World Records* at the time.

A few years later Irving Langmuir, a New York-born physicist and Nobel Prize winner in Chemistry, said this was tosh. In more scientific terms, he said that to achieve this speed, the fly would have to eat one-and-a-half times its own weight every second. Even more highly unlikely. Langmuir then calculated that, at over 1,000 kilometres per hour, the fly would be invisible to the human eye, but producing an audible sonic boom and almost two atmospheres of air pressure – enough to crush the insect's head and cause gunshot-grade trauma if it collided with any kind of body. Clearly, this is not what Townsend saw on the hillside in New Mexico (even if the deer bots had been going that fast, he wouldn't have been able to see them; plus he would probably have been too distracted by the sonic boom to look).

This is not to say that the deer botfly is slow. It's simply slower than the speed of sound. Quite a bit slower. Langmuir's last word on the subject was that its real speed is more likely around 40 kilometres per hour, although some more recent tests put it closer to 80 kilometres per hour.

It's clear that flies are fast fliers. But no one's really sure exactly how fast. Insect speeds in general are misunderstood and often mismeasured. Far too few have been firmly enough confirmed to say conclusively who's faster than who. But the male horsefly is still thought to be the fastest. This was confirmed by Jerry Butler, an entomologist from the University of Florida, who once got one to chase and catch a plastic pellet fired from an air rifle. From this he calculated that the boy horse fly was flying at speeds of at least 145 kilometres per hour. That's hard to beat, especially considering that the average speed of a fly in flight (like a housefly) is closer to seven or eight kilometres per hour.

5. Landing on the ceiling

It's one of those eternal questions that has bugged people almost as much as flies have. How does a fly land upside down on the ceiling – especially considering that it's flying right-way-up until all but the last moment?

It's a question that's bugged scientists too. So much so that they have studied it. For years, the prevalent theory was that flies use a fighter-pilot-style barrel roll to flip over sidewards when coming in to land. But the debate raged on until 1945 when high-speed photography and freeze frames allowed scientists to take an even closer, slow-motion look.

The answer? It's not a flip, but a flop – more along the lines of an acrobat's somersault than a pilot's roll. Just before landing, the still right-way-up fly extends its front legs over its head to touch the ceiling. It gets a good grip, and then uses momentum from the fly-up to flop the rest of its body and feet over its head, upside down and onto the surface above. Gymnasts are thought to do similar twists on the uneven bars. But they can't do it upside down.

6. Walking on the ceiling

Landing is one thing. Stopping, staying and strolling around up there calls for even more skill. A fly doesn't weigh much – between 10 to 15 milligrams – but defying gravity is still something of a challenge. It calls for a fine balance between body weight and surface adhesion – too much of either and you're either falling fast or sticking hard. The same applies to walking on slippery vertical surfaces like window panes and well-scrubbed bathroom tiles, which flies can do too (much to the chagrin of the person who's just finished scrubbing).

> Scientists have shown that, to land upside down on a ceiling, a fly does not a flip, but a flop. More like an acrobat's forward somersault than a pilot's sideward roll.

Fortunately, the fly is blessed with gravity-defying footwear. It has two soft, sticky pads called pulvilli on each foot, which provide the kind of

> Getting stuck on the ceiling is clearly not the goal, so the fly's feet also come with two counteracting claws to help pull each foot free.

active adhesive surface area to which Spiderman and Lionel Richie (famed singer of songs about dancing on the ceiling) would both aspire. The pads also come with tiny, round-tipped hairs called setae that help with grip and secrete an oily kind of glue composed of sugars and fats.

The result is a super-sticky situation, which could get even stickier if the pulvilli and setae were too effective. Getting stuck upside down is clearly not the goal, so the fly's feet also come with two counteracting claws to help pull the foot free. This was confirmed by a team from the Max Planck Institute for Metals Research in Germany who investigated more than 300 wall-climbing insects and the sticky footprints they left behind. They also found that flies physically push, twist and peel their footpads free – with peeling being the most effective release option.

The research didn't stop there. The Max Planck contingent then collaborated with a robotics team from Case Western Reserve University in Cleveland, Ohio, USA, who were designing fly-like feet for a leggy 85 gram robot. They covered the robot's feet in a synthetic hairy, sticky material and even programmed it to peel its foot off a glass wall, just like the real thing. The robot managed pretty well. Not the first time something has been driven up the wall by a fly.

7. Leg rubbing

No, they are not hatching plans to take over the world. But flies do spend a lot of time rubbing their legs together with apparent glee. In reality, they are simply cleaning themselves. They have to. And so would you if your body was covered with hairs that function as touch, smell and taste receptors (see point 2), but that are constantly being trailed across rubbish dumps and dung heaps.

It's like nose blowing. The fly has to clean itself if it wants to smell and taste what it's about to eat. But there might be more to it than that. It's thought that female flies groom more than males and that all flies groom more in the presence of other flies. Read into that what you will.

> The fly has to rub its legs together because they are covered with hairs that function as smell and taste receptors. It's like nose blowing. It has to clean itself if it wants to smell and taste what it's about to eat.

Fly grooming is quite a clever process – so clever that scientists have spent lots of time and money on it. Even Richard Dawkins (yes, *the* Richard Dawkins, British evolutionary biologist extraordinaire) has turned his mind to the topic. In 1976, he and fellow researcher Marian Dawkins (who also happens to be his wife) published a full report on the rules governing fly grooming. Another study from the University of Massachusetts, published in 1993 in Genetics, summarises these rules as follows:

> The leg movements used to clean a particular body area are highly stereotyped, consisting of patterned leg-sweeping movements followed by a series of leg-rubbing movements. Initially, a leg sweeps a portion of the body, such as the head, wing or notum (top of the thorax). The leg is then rubbed against another leg ... to remove the accumulated debris. Cleaning of a particular body part is achieved by repeated bouts of leg sweeping and rubbing. The eyes and spiracles tend to be cleaned first followed by the wings, notum and abdomen.

This refers specifically to the fruit fly, but we have all seen the housefly and many other species do much the same thing. Put more simply, the fly first uses one front or back leg to rub a body part clean. Then the other front or rear leg is brought in to scrape down its now dirty match. For some reason, the middle two legs aren't used for cleaning, although they do get cleaned. That's why you're unlikely to see a fly rubbing its middle pair of legs together – which would probably be impossible or just look rather odd.

For some reason, the middle two legs aren't used for cleaning, although they do get cleaned. That's why you're unlikely to see a fly rubbing its middle pair of legs together.

According to the University of Massachusetts study quoted above, flies actually don't groom all that much. Unless you sprinkle them with dust, that is. Which the researchers really did. After being dusted, the flies immediately spent about three times more time grooming than the dust-free controls. They also performed more grooming behaviour when certain specific tactile hairs were stimulated. Which the researchers did too.

It's all in a day's work: watching flies land on ceilings, pulling, pushing and moving their hairs, covering their bodies with chalk dust and watching how they rub themselves clean. Who says scientists are boring? Their fascination with flies truly knows no bounds.

FLY IN MEDICINE

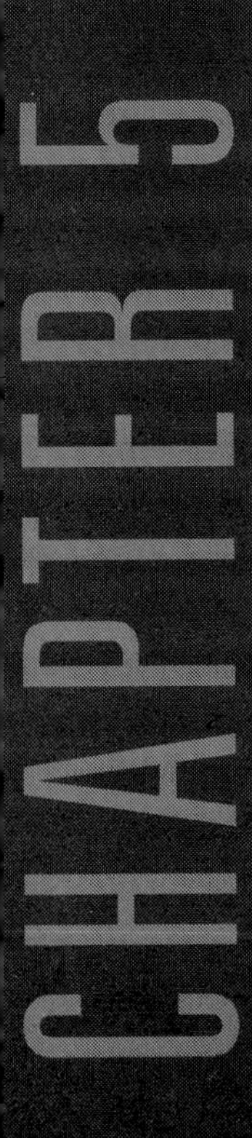

IF THEY GAVE MEDALS to insects, fly larvae would have more than most. They would be wriggling around on well-decorated chests, dragging their metalwork through the mud and muck. Some kind of Napoleonic sign of distinction, a Congressional Medal of Honour for the American Civil War perhaps, or a Distinguished Service Cross for World War I. Amongst others.

That's a lot of metal to pin on a small, squishy, soft-centred creature. But each medal would be well won and more than well deserved. Larvae have been accidental war heroes since Genghis Kahn got busy conquering Eurasia in the early 1200s. His armies travelled with cartloads of flies, whose larvae they used to clean and disinfect their soldiers' wounds. Far from being medically backward, this was in fact quite forward-looking. Larvae are once again being used in hospitals today -- as you will soon see.

Genghis Kahn's armies travelled with cartloads of flies, whose larvae they used to disinfect their soldiers' wounds. Larvae are once again being used in hospitals today.

You will also see that, simply by going about the business of feeding on rotten things, larvae can help people get better faster. That's certainly worth an honourable mention or two. Like this one, by Napoleon Bonaparte's Surgeon-in-Chief, Baron Dominique Jean Larrey:

> These insects, so far from being injurious to [soldiers'] wounds, promoted rather their cicatrisation by cutting short the process of nature ... These larvae are indeed greedy only after putrefying substances and never touched the parts endowed with life.

That's a Neoclassical way of saying that fly larvae will clean out dead or damaged tissue while leaving the healthy bits behind. This is not to say that the Baron actually applied the maggots to wounded soldiers himself. He didn't. But he did observe that, when they infested of their own accord, the larvae somehow reduced infection and promoted healing. Much to surgeon and soldier's amazement and relief.

Modern scientists and doctors feel the same way. That's why they will go so far as to buy in bottles of sterile maggots from specialised suppliers and spoon them into suppurating diabetic ulcers and other stubborn infections and injuries. And patients allow it. They swallow their doubts and choke on the revulsion that's instinctively linked to thoughts of writhing, flesh-eating things. They turn their heads away, but still allow spoonfuls of maggots to be placed inside the infected parts of their bodies and covered over with special dressings so that they can't escape. Then they go home for a couple of days and try not to think about what's going on under that neat square of gauze. They allow it because they are desperate. But also because it works. Especially when all else fails.

After only four weeks of maggot therapy, non-healing diabetic leg ulcers were completely debrided, or free of any tissue that was infected, damaged or dead.

In fact, according to 2003 research by Dr Ronald A Sherman, clinical myiasis or maggot infestation is a more effective treatment for non-healing diabetic foot and leg ulcers than less gruesome, conventional therapies. After five weeks of conventional treatment, Sherman found that ulcers were still 33 percent covered with dead tissue, but after only four weeks of maggot therapy, they had healed better and were completely debrided, or free of anything infected, damaged or dead.

It's simple, really. Larvae only like things putrid and pus-filled. They will always pick the infected or rotten over anything good, clean and fresh. In fact, they cannot eat undamaged cells at all. Hence their preference for corpses and decaying food, and their ability to stop debriding wounds when only the hale and healthy tissue remains.

Clearly, myiasis is a grisly process, but it helps wounds get much less grisly much more quickly. That's why Ronald Sherman has spent so many years becoming the global go-to guy for Maggot Debridement Therapy, or MDT. He is a physician, researcher and co-founder and laboratory director at medical maggot supplier, Monarch Labs in Irvine,

California. In short, he loves maggots, or rather loves what they can do, namely: 1) clean wounds by dissolving infected and dead tissue; 2) disinfect the area by killing bacteria; and 3) actively accelerate the healing process. And these days Sherman isn't the only one loving larvae's three-in-one, wound-care plan. In 1995, only a handful of practitioners in four countries were using MDT; today there are over 4,000 therapists active in 20 countries or more.

The official signing and sealing came in 2004. That was when the US Food and Drug Administration (FDA) approved the production and prescription of a specific strain of green blowfly, *Phaenicia sericata*, larvae for medical use. In the same year, the British National Health Service (NHS) also approved the use of MDT within its public hospital walls. And so maggots wormed their way into the mainstream. Just four years later, in 2008, it was estimated that a total of 50,000 courses of MDT were dispensed to around 10,000 patients worldwide.

In 1995, a handful of practitioners were using Maggot Debridement Therapy. By 2008 an estimated 50,000 courses of treatment were dispensed to 10,000 patients worldwide.

THE PAST

It hasn't always been this way. Over hundreds or even thousands of years, MDT research and development crawled along as slowly as a maggot crawling along without anything dead or dying to eat. There are a few moments of recorded maggot-driven debridement – by the Mayans, for instance, as well as certain Aboriginal tribes and a few progressive sorts during the Renaissance. But, generally, humans have always been maggot-shy – it's hard not to be when nature has taught us to associate these creatures with death and decay, not healing and health. As a result, maggot therapy has a long history of unproven, infrequent and mostly accidental use. Unsurprisingly, most of this happened during wars, like the Napoleonic Wars and the American Civil War.

It was a horrible, harrowing war that ravaged America during the early 1860s. Union soldiers from the North and Confederate from the South injured and slaughtered each other in droves. Bodies piled up. Flesh festered. When the maggots moved in to eat, doctors welcomed them into open wounds with open arms.

> 'Maggots ... in a single day would clean a wound much better than any agents we had at our command' — Dr J F Zacharias, American Civil War medical officer

'Maggots ... in a single day would clean a wound much better than any agents we had at our command,' said Dr J F Zacharias, a now famous Confederate medical officer. 'I am sure I saved many lives by their use,' he is quoted as saying. He is also credited as being the first modern-era doctor to actively use maggots therapeutically. And so did Confederate medical officer Dr Joseph Jones, who reported: '... as far as my experience extends, these worms only destroy dead tissues, and do not injure specifically the well parts.'

The American Civil War battlefields are still considered the birthplace of modern maggot therapy – the intentional kind.

But it wasn't until World War I that the so-called father of modern maggot therapy stepped up to the plate to parent his brood. He was William Baer, clinical professor of orthopaedic surgery at Johns Hopkins University in Baltimore, Maryland. During the War, as men shot at each other in teeming trenches, Baer noticed that soldiers left lying on the battlefield for days would be found with maggot-packed wounds but none of the fever, pus or systemic infection that their injuries would suggest. He was surprised. On seeing one such case – complete with compound fractures and maggoty flesh wounds – Baer noted that 'there was practically no bare bone to be seen and the internal structure of the wounded bone as well as the surrounding parts was entirely covered with the most beautiful pink tissue that one could imagine' Beautiful, pink, healthy, healing tissue. Not just surprised, Baer was also inspired.

After the War he got to work breeding flies in a lab. He then went in search of more beautiful, pink, healthy tissue at Baltimore's Children's Hospital. Here he used larvae to successfully treat up to 100 children with osteomyelitis and soft-tissue infections. He presented the findings at a 1929 surgical conference, but they were published only two years later and, unfortunately, posthumously.

Along the way Baer realised that maggots can be dirty or clean, dangerous or safe. His unsterilised stock did help to heal wounds within six weeks. But when he applied them to more patients, some developed tetanus – an unfortunate complication leading to the fortunate conclusion that `safe' maggots need to be sterile and germ-free. The trend was set. Throughout the 1930s, sterile maggots were increasingly used in the US on wounds and burns by thousands of practitioners and institutions. This continued into the 1940s until penicillin and other antibiotics and surgical techniques pushed MDT off the top of the heap of things medically bizarre. During the decades that followed, that is where it stayed – to be pulled out only occasionally when desperate times called for measures to match.

Now we know how it all works. No longer a mysterious and seemingly medieval intervention, MDT has been investigated and explained by a substance called allantoin. Fly larvae secrete it, and it also occurs naturally in the herb comfrey, wheat sprouts, tobacco seeds and horse chestnut bark. This skin-soothing compound has been found to actively stimulate healing and cell proliferation. More recent research shows that the effective molecule in allantoin is in fact urea. That is why allantoin and urea have frequently been used in the treatment of resistant ulcers and wounds. They have also found their way into shaving gels and various skin- and oral-care products. Perhaps not as effective as maggots. But certainly easier to package and apply.

Fly larvae secrete allantoin, a skin-soothing compound that stimulates healing and repair. It also occurs naturally in the herb comfrey, a more common skin treatment.

The question is, which would you prefer: having a few hundred fly larvae spread onto your skin, or sitting in a closed shed with a trough full of dead animals crawling with larvae too? It's a tough choice, and luckily one you wouldn't have to make unless you had some kind of supurative ulcer or pulmonary TB. Also, you would have to be living in West Yorkshire, England, in the early 1900s. That was when Arthur Bryant made a name for himself farming maggots for fishing bait and curing cases of tuberculosis in sheds on the side.

> Every week in summer, meat was boiled and taken into the woods to gather larvae. Then the meat and maggots were transferred to enclosed sheds where inhalation therapy patients sat around talking and playing cards.

He called himself the Maggot King, and he called his farm the Maggotorium. As catchy as the condition he purported to cure, Bryant's chosen names stuck and consumptives came from across the Yorkshire area for a course of the controversial maggot inhalation therapy. Bryant himself was proof that it worked – he, too, had suffered from TB and at one point was even denied life insurance as a result. But, after just a few months of farming maggots and breathing in their fumes, he was granted both improved health and £200 worth of life cover. Clearly there was something in the air at the Maggotorium. Something very good.

Topical maggot therapy was already known to medicine, so it wasn't such a crazy concept. But it was a crazy set-up. Every week in the summer, four to five tonnes of deceased zoo-animal meat was boiled in boiling sheds and then taken into the woods to gather larvae. Then the meat and maggots were transferred to tin baths in enclosed sheds. Here they were left to eat, grow and emit fumes for groups of inhalation therapy patients who sat around talking, playing cards and just breathing everything in.

Despite the card games and good conversation, it couldn't have been much fun. It's said that the smell of the place was discernible almost five kilometres away. But sick people who want to get better will tolerate all kinds of discomforts. And these very sick, and very tolerant, people really did get very much better.

'I weighed eight stone, nine pounds when I went to the Maggotorium and after four weeks I weighed nine stone,' said one testimonial on a brochure produced by Bryant. 'My appetite is much better and I can breathe more freely. My cough is almost gone, except first thing in the morning.'

'At the present time I am feeling splendid, and can truly testify to the benefit obtained by undergoing the treatment,' said another content consumptive. 'I have been in another sanatorium but received no benefit thereby ... after six weeks of Mr Bryant's treatment I was able to resume my ordinary duties.'

That's splendid indeed. And science says so too. Even back then, a local Bradford city analyst confirmed that maggot gases contain ammonia and two amine compounds called dimethylamine and trimethylamine – a combination that's responsible for a characteristic smell of ammonia and fish. But it's also responsible for larvae fumes' antimicrobial and healing properties. At the time ammonia was already a known antiseptic and trimethylamine was also used successfully to treat pneumonia, cholera and arthritis. So it all made sense to the Bradford city analyst who promptly recommended that the positive results be released to the public. But they weren't. And maggot inhalation therapy is still waiting for its moment in the sun.

Fly larvae fumes contain ammonia – a known antiseptic – and two amine compounds, one of which has been used to treat pneumonia, cholera and arthritis.

Despite his anecdotal success, Arthur Bryant never got to open the more formal, medical Maggotorium of his dreams. But that didn't stop him from trying. By 1939 he had moved to Buckinghamshire where he kept farming maggots and advertising himself as the Maggot King of Buckingham'. Poor Bryant. He had to toot his own horn because clearly no one else would. Maggot inhalation therapy might have been supported by science, but it was still snubbed by the snot-nosed medical mores of the time.

'Since there is increasing evidence that the tubercular bacillus will eventually become resistant to all current antibiotics ... Perhaps we have not seen the last of maggot inhalation therapy.'
— Dr Milton Wainwright, University of Sheffield

'It should be remembered that during the 1930s, the British medical authorities were antagonistic to the use of maggot therapy on wounds and burns, despite the fact that this method was widely used with great effect in the US,' writes Sheffield University's Dr Milton Wainwright in a 2007 feature in the journal Microbiologist. He goes on to explain that, despite its apparent medical merits, maggot inhalation therapy was canned by conservative practitioners. A real pity – particularly because Wainwright's own modern research supports these merits.

In 1988 Dr Wainwright and his team published research showing that fumes produced by various species of fly larvae can inhibit the growth of the bacterium *Mycobacterium phlei*. This noninfectious organism is from the same greater family as TB-causing *Mycobacterium tuberculosis*. In fact, it's often used by scientists as a research proxy for its more risky tubercular relative. The fact that larvae fumes can hinder *M. phlei* is clearly an encouraging piece of science. One that suggests the maggot shed may not have breathed its last.

'Since there is increasing evidence that the tubercular bacillus will eventually become resistant to all current antibiotics, we may yet have to resort to other therapies,' Wainwright explains. 'Perhaps we have not seen the last of maggot inhalation therapy,' he continues. You can almost hear the smile in his words.

THE PRESENT

'Maggots may not be applied more than once. 'Used' maggots must be handled as contaminated medical waste; unused maggots must be destroyed.' — Medical Maggots™ package insert

It's quite simple really. Let's say you're a doctor and you place an order with Medical Maggots™ online. Your Standard Vial will arrive, containing about 1,000 sterilised blowfly eggs that will yield 250 to 500 maggots within about 12 hours. The vial also comes with a piece of gauze and some soy protein and brewer's yeast to act as a food source when the hatchlings appear. That's all for the low, low price of just under $100. Or you could opt for the Large Vial and get double the number of larvae for only $50 more. Either way, this is a disposable or 'single use only item', the package insert warns: '... maggots may not be applied more than once. 'Used' maggots must be handled as contaminated medical waste; unused maggots must be destroyed.'

According to the greatest MD in MDT, Monarch Labs' Ronald Sherman, the first modern clinical investigations into Maggot Debridement Therapy started in 1989 in California. The aim was to establish: 1) if MDT is still useful today; 2) whether it compares well to other treatments; and 3) if it should be considered as more than just a last resort.

The answers were yes, yes and yes, respectively.

Sherman's research, performed at California's Veterans Affairs Medical Center and the University of California, found that maggot therapy was not only safe, effective (and cost-effective), but also that, while 'pre-amputation MDT' has a limb-salvage rate of more than 40 percent, this can be even higher when used earlier in treatment. In other words, not just when all other options have been exhausted and the idea of flesh-eating maggots has lost some of its sting.

Research shows that 'pre-amputation Maggot Debridement Therapy' has a limb-salvage rate of more than 40 percent. This can be even higher when used earlier in treatment.

Problem is, MDT is still largely a bottom-of-the-barrel treatment. It works, but it scares people. Maybe things haven't changed much in over 100 years. Sherman thinks the problem still lies with fly larvae PR. In response to the assumption that most patients don't want these creepy-crawlies on their bodies, he writes:

> 'What patients do not want is a stinking, draining wound. What patients do not want is to lose their foot. What patients do not want is four more weeks of a treatment in which they do not see any benefit. Wearing 'baby flies' for two days is not too high a price to pay, if the potential for success is what is reported with MDT.'

Perhaps MDT simply needs some creative rebranding. 'Baby fly therapy' has a much more marketable ring to it. That said, humans throughout history and across the globe have tolerated all sorts of creepy-crawly nastiness in the interest of better health. Baby flies are in baby class. In fact, insect interventions can be far nastier than MDT, depending on the species of 'practitioner' and the practice itself.

Case in point: the Spanish fly, which incidentally is not a fly, but a special kind of blister beetle. In the past the beetle's wings were used to make blister-raising plasters – and yes, people really wore them. Nowadays its blood is a commercial source of the blistering agent cantharidin – and people use it to treat urogenital and kidney infections, benign growths like warts, and as a mating stimulant in animal husbandry (and some misguided human husbandry, too).

Even more invasive than a beetle-blood blistering agent, consider the soldier-ant stitches used in India, South America and the Middle East. Large-jawed ants are encouraged to bite down on opposing edges of a flesh wound. Then their bodies are pinched off leaving a neat row of heads to hold everything together. Ouch!

'What patients do not want is a stinking, draining wound. What patients do not want is to lose their foot. Wearing 'baby flies' for two days is not too high a price to pay.' — Dr Ronald Sherman

But at least that's still external. Historically, spiders have been swallowed and bedbug broth has been drunk to treat malaria. Grasshoppers have been taken for seizures. Today, in parts of Europe, powdered cockroaches can be bought as an oral treatment for inflammation around the heart or lungs. But that's nothing. Most invasive of all is probably bee or wasp-sting therapy, which claims that multiple, controlled stings can help treat arthritis, multiple sclerosis and even certain cancers. And it's not just the beekeepers who believe. The patients keep coming. So there is hope for maggots' medical reputation yet.

At least MDT doesn't hurt. It shouldn't, because larvae are so small they usually can't even be felt moving around in a wound. They also can't bite because they don't have teeth. They do, however, have mouth hooks and rough bumps on their bodies, which help them grab, tear and move through dead tissue with ease. This is all good for the patient too. In fact the hooks and bumps help the larvae to more effectively debride the tissue they are traversing – along with the digestive, liquefying enzymes they release to break things down before sucking them back up.

Fly larvae make natural nurses for non-healing wounds. The way they eat and move serves to help the nursing along. But, even if you manage to explain all of this to your patient – and to convince her that MDT is nowhere near as nasty as roach powder or wasp stings – there are still some technical problems to solve. Like the openness of the 'open' ulcer or wound you are trying to heal.

Remember that in nature maggots will eat until satiated and then wander off to find a burrow where they can pupate. But this isn't nature, and these maggots are needed on-site and on the job. So, as doctor (and slave-driver) you would need to seal them inside the wound with tape and a porous, 'cage-like' dressing that allows maggots to move around, air to come in and liquefied tissue and secretions to drain out.

Once this is done, your patient and her strapped-in passengers can usually be sent home for a day or two. During this time, the larvae will deliver around-the-clock, at-home care. All they need is a bit of air to breathe and enough dead, damaged or infected tissue to keep feeding, both of which are readily available. But, as soon as they are done slaving away at eating and secreting (usually within 48 to 72 hours), the larvae will instinctively make a quick crawl for freedom. This is why the dressing should be removed after 48 hours or so – any longer and the risk of runaways increases considerably.

> 'Beware: Escaping maggots may upset the staff and/ or hospital administrators'
> — Medical Maggots™ package insert

'Beware: Escaping maggots may upset the staff and/or hospital administrators,' the Medical Maggots™ package insert warns again. 'Upset' is probably an understatement. But at this stage in the treatment, the larval wanderlust can actually work in both doctor and patient's favour. Why? Because there is no danger of any stragglers getting lost or left behind inside the wound – another scare story for potential patients of MDT. In fact the maggots will probably be waiting at the gate when you peel the dressing from the wound. Any dawdlers and slow-growers can be washed or wiped out with ease. And another batch can be brought in if necessary.

And so it goes. Apply. Cover. Remove. Repeat. After one to six cycles of MDT, your patient's ulcer will be pink, healthy and debrided enough to cover over or graft. There will be hugs, flowers and kudos for you, the daring and progressive doctor. But the real heroes are the fly larvae, now used-up, washed-out and destined for disposal as medical waste.

THE FUTURE

Just by reading this you are becoming part of the maggots' medical public relations plan. You are probably beginning to like them a little more. At some point you may even start to see them as brilliant baby flies – which would bode very well for more medical maggot success. The only thing standing in their way is the stubborn human tendency to think they are gross.

But there is also a growing group of go-getters and game-changers who don't think maggots are gross at all. People like the larvae farmers at AgriProtein (whom you will get to know better in later chapters of this book). And also Gunter Pauli, an entrepreneur and author of *The Blue Economy – 10 years, 100 innovations, 100 million jobs*, who calls them 'Nature's Nurses' and places them second on his list of 100 innovations that will help reduce waste, promote health and shape a more sustainable (or blue) economy.

> Wound treatment for a leg ulcer can cost about $2,000 per patient. That's not even a diabetic foot ulcer, which can drain the health-care system of an estimated $30,000.

These blue-sky thinkers see fly larvae as a source of untapped environmental and economic potential. There are real-world numbers to support this view: according to Pauli, wound treatment for a leg ulcer can cost about $2,000 per patient – and that's not even a diabetic foot ulcer, which can drain the health-care system of an estimated $30,000. Clearly, farmed medical maggots – or products containing their extracted proteolytic enzymes – could help to save society countless dollars, lives and limbs. Especially now that we know exactly how these natural nurses work.

'Now that we understand the 'mechanism of maggots' we are translating this knowledge to make effective wound-care products,' University of Nottingham School of Pharmacy researcher David Pritchard told National Geographic News in June 2009. The potential products include gels or bandages impregnated with 'maggot-juice' – 'an enzyme from the maggot fluid with the capacity to remove decaying tissue from the wound, giving the underlying tissue a better chance to heal'.

> Potential wound-care products include gels or bandages impregnated with 'maggot-juice' – an enzyme from the larval fluid with the capacity to remove decaying tissue.

The continuous research and development is a big pat on the back for medical maggots and the juices they generate. But is it enough? Will the powers-that-be be prepared to invest in the industry and pay for the treatments that result?

'It's strange,' says Dr Ronald Sherman, 'but some insurance companies will pay tens of thousands of dollars for an amputation, probably because it is so common nowadays, but will hesitate or object to paying $100 for a course of maggot therapy, even though studies repeatedly demonstrate that medicinal maggots have saved 40 to 50 percent of limbs otherwise scheduled for amputation due to non-healing wounds.'

Again this comes down to attitude. It's strange indeed, and also a little short-sighted. Which is why Sherman is also now acting as director of the BioTherapeutics, Education & Research (BTER) Foundation, established in California in 2003 to champion a menagerie of 'biotherapists' like maggots, leeches, honey bees, 'doctor fish', therapeutic worms, sniffer dogs, horses and other domestic animals and pets. 'Saving Lives, Saving Limbs, Every Day, Nature's Way.' That's the organisation's tag line. It works towards this aim by supporting biotherapeutic care, education and research. But also by helping patients without sufficient health insurance to pay for the treatments they need.

That said and despite Sherman's concerns, in 2008 the American Medical Association and the US Centers for Medicare and Medicaid Services released clearer, simpler guidelines for maggot therapy reimbursement. This means it's getting increasingly easier for patients to be treated and doctors then to be paid.

It's a work-in-progress, but it does mean that MDT is becoming mainstream enough for risk-takers and rule-makers alike.

Yet another pat on the back for the brilliant baby flies. Or a medal on the chest, depending on which side is facing up.

Some insurance companies will pay tens of thousands of dollars for an amputation, probably because it is so common nowadays, but will hesitate to pay $100 for a course of maggot therapy.

CHAPTER 6

FLY AS FLYING MACHINE

THE WORD 'FLY' is a verb. But it's also a noun, which is potentially confusing. Especially when you're shooing one with an irate, "Fly away fly!" It's hard to establish precisely which of these two identical F-words is the noun and which is the verb. Although it doesn't matter, really. Either could be either. And the very fact that the words are so easily interchangeable tells us something about the insect that's earned the verb as a noun for a name.

It could have been called a 'flier'. That would more than adequately express what this creature can naturally do. Someone who runs well or often is known as a runner, not a run. Someone who builds well is a builder. Someone who sings well is called a singer, not a song.

But calling a fly a fly is tantamount to saying that this insect is absolutely defined by what it does. Why? Because it flies better than it does anything else.

If your brief is to build an unmanned, insect-sized craft that can swoop into remote areas to observe without being observed itself, then you'd best start investigating the unmanned insect that spends its life doing just that.

The name is a handy hint for anyone interested in the ins and outs of flight. Think about it: if you're an aerodynamic engineer investigating flight and designing airborne machines, you'd best start looking at the creature that bears the action as a name. And, if your brief is to build an unmanned, insect sized craft that can swoop into remote areas to observe without being observed, then you'd best start with the insect that spends its life doing just that. Which is exactly what a subset of aerodynamic engineers are doing – particularly those at work on micro air vehicles, or MAVs.

Some MAVs are hobby projects designed for competitive aerial robotics or photography. Others are for more serious missions – like search-and-rescue operations and military espionage stings. Of course, snooping behind enemy lines is far safer for a camera-packing insect-bot than a large aircraft full of soldiers. That's why big-gun groups like NASA, the US Department of Defense and the Defense Advance Research Projects Agency (DARPA) are spending millions of dollars on sourcing the ultimate aerodynamic, sensing and data-processing functions for their fly-on-the-wall machines.

It's called bioinspiration – sometimes biomimicry – the process of mimicking nature to solve design problems and inspire human invention. Historically, flies have been big bioinspirers. Hieroglyphics from as far back as 1650 BC depict their flying talents as linked to the pharaohs' flight to the hereafter. Similarly, ancient Roman and Syrian engravings make mention of the airborne overachievers. And, in more modern times, so does the work of Michael Dickinson, professor of Bioengineering at the California Institute of Technology.

'[Flies are] nature's fighter jets ... arguably the most aerodynamically sophisticated of all flying animals' — Professor Michael Dickinson, fly bioengineer, California Institute of Technology

'The success of flies is due in part to their many specialisations for flight,' writes fly expert Dickinson (also known less officially as the Flyman, as you may recall from Chapter 4). He explains that, when in hot pursuit of a hot female, the male fly has been found to change direction in fewer than 30 milliseconds. 'This is extraordinarily fast processing,' he says, 'and illustrates why the flight system of flies represents the gold standard for flying machines.'

Dickinson is going for this gold standard by cutting and pasting skills from the fly's natural world into our unnatural one. He is a firm believer in using the best biomimics to develop the best flying machines and airborne devices. Like proposed MAVs, which 'would weigh less than a ballpoint pen and fit comfortably in a coffee cup', says Dickinson, 'a description that also fits most of the six million or so species of insects on the planet'. Most importantly the fly. Of course.

THE SCI-FI OF HOW FLIES FLY

According to Michael Dickinson, flies are 'nature's fighter jets' . He also says they are 'arguably the most aerodynamically sophisticated of all flying animals'. This attitude, supported by years of research, has earned this Flyman the (more official) title of `fly bioengineer'. Just in case that didn't go to his head, he was also granted an award that dubs him an (equally official) `genius', the MacArthur Fellowship that Dickinson received in 2001 -- along with $500,000. Hard to say which part of the prize is worth more.

When he got the phone call that the Fellowship was his, Dickinson was hiking through dense Hawaiian guava forests in search of wild swarms of fruit flies. He is said to have scratched the Foundation's phone number in the sand with a stick. Sounds like an Indiana Jones movie. But most of Dickinson's life and work reads more like sci-fi than an adventure scene.

One such scene co-stars Dickinson and Robofly – a scaled Plexiglas model of a fruit fly suspended in a vat of mineral oil. Three motors on each wing power flapping motion in all directions and in rotation. Sensors are attached to measure the forces generated. All-in-all, this makes Robofly an action superstar who does his own stunts and charts his own progress. But he also helps Dickinson and team to take fly flight to even greater heights.

Robofly is an action star who does his own stunts. He is a Plexiglas fruit fly in a vat of mineral oil. He has a half-metre wingspan and three motors that flap each wing in all directions and in rotation.

'Most aeronautic engineers take large airplanes and model them as small things in a wind tunnel,' writes Dickinson. 'We take a tiny fly and model it as a giant thing in 200 metric tons of mineral oil.' The result? This oversize, robotic, floating fly has allowed the team to distil the real fly's high-speed flapping into three distinct wing movements that drive the insect's every acrobatic trick and manoeuvre.

The fly's flapping has been distilled into three distinct wing movements that drive every aerobatic manoeuvre. These movements are shared by almost every other insect. And the hummingbird – an 'honorary insect' when it comes to flight.

In fact, although they differ from those used by airplanes and most birds, these wing movements seem to be shared by just about every other kind of insect. As well as the hummingbird – considered an 'honorary insect' when it comes to matters of flapping and flight.

The ideal futuristic action hero with heart, Robofly has a half-metre wingspan and a will to solve the problems that plague humankind. Problems like: How do flies really fly? And: Can we use their skills to help fight wars and save the world?

'Although a bit messy, Robofly has proven to be a scientifically very productive instrument,' Dickinson continues. Why? Because 'even brute-force mathematical computations on supercomputers cannot accurately predict the forces created by a flapping wing'. Not that the Flyman is averse to supercomputers and complex computations. No, not at all. Firstly, they are less messy. And, secondly, what's a good sci-fi without some gadgets, mathematical equations and convoluted tech-speak thrown in for good measure?

Think about it: if you want to calculate and compute the system behind an insect's impressive skills in flight, you need a tool with which to simulate and observe those skills before getting down to the numbers they involve. That's where the lab's two flight simulators come in -- the Fly-O-Rama and Rock-n-Roll Arena. Fly-O-Rama is a detailed motion-tracking tool – a large cylinder lined with 12,000 computer-controlled, light-emitting diodes (LEDs). Everything about this device is designed to create the illusion of flight. It's like virtual reality for flies, but without the funny glasses.

First the chosen fruit fly is placed inside the cylinder, often glued to a thin wire and tied to a steel rod. A small piece of paper simulates take-off from firm ground. 'When we're ready to start, we blow the paper away,' writes Dickinson. 'Tiny touch sensors on the [fly's] legs detect the loss of terra firma, and the fly begins to fly. We can stop each experiment by carefully replacing the piece of paper. The fly's legs sense the contact and trigger the wings to stop.' So simple and so clever. The fly flies on the spot and the scientists can assess every move. Even more clever, a splash of sugar water on the landing paper triggers taste cells on the fly's feet for a quick feed between flights.

But Fly-O-Rama is more than just a paper-pushing, food-dispensing, virtual fly-flying machine. Following pseudo-take-off, the fly pseudo-soars past the 12,000 LEDs, displaying a pseudo-changing environment made up of shifting squares and stripes. 'We can measure the fly's intended flight behaviour by tracking the motion of its wings with an optical wingbeat analyzer, or by fixing the fly to a sensitive torque meter,' says Dickinson. The scientists and supercomputers are watching every move. In fact they are watching the fly watching the changing landscape and moving in response too.

It's like hand-eye coordination. Or rather, wing-eye coordination. Dickinson's team has established that flies fly in short straight lines broken by changes in direction called `saccades'. These saccades see the fly shift 90° in less than the blink of an eye – actually in eight wing strokes or 30 to 50 milliseconds. Literally faster than a human eye could ever hope to open, shut and open again. But it's the fly's eyes that trigger each blinking fast turn. That's what Fly-O-Rama's changing wallpaper patterns have helped to show.

Flies can change direction by 90° in less than the blink of an eye – actually in eight wing strokes or 30 to 50 milliseconds, which is literally faster than a human eye could ever hope to open, shut and open again.

'By carefully measuring the animal's flight path in Fly-O-Rama, we can reconstruct the visual world from the fly's perspective,' says

Dickinson, 'the equivalent of sitting on the back of the fly as it zips around the arena.'

The result? In addition to motion sickness, this fake fly rodeo ride has given the researchers an idea of what causes the buck and shift through each 90° saccade – namely an 'expansion of the fly's visual world', says Dickinson. 'These saccades are collision-avoidance reflexes that keep the animal from crashing into objects.' Thank you Fly-O-Rama. We may not have needed you to tell us that a fruit fly will change direction to dodge a crash. But it does help to understand how sophisticated this insect's aerosensory system really is. Which means it's time to look a little deeper into their eyes.

THE SCI-FI OF HOW FLIES SEE

'If you take a fly on a date to the movies it will think you brought it to a slide show,' says Dickinson. He explains that, although fruit flies aren't so sharp when it comes to image-forming and spatial resolution – at just 25 x 25 pixels per eye, they lag pitifully behind the 1000 x 1000 pixels of a cheap digital camera – their temporal resolution allows them to resolve flashing lights up to 10 times faster than we can.

About two-thirds of the fly brain is reserved for processing information and images that their over-active eyes can see.

So, in addition to making them bad movie dates, fly eyes also help to make the insects masters of flight. This is why about two-thirds of the fly brain is reserved for processing what their overactive eyes can see. But that's still not enough information. When you're trying to get a full view of how the creature named after its greatest skill performs, you need more pictures of more parts of the process. Which probably means you need some more machines.

The so-called Rock-n-Roll Arena is a machine that provides a second layer of flight simulation for Dickinson's lab. It's a big metal frame or gimbal designed to hold a large arena that holds a fly. Once suspended within the frame, both arena and fly can be spun in various directions around various axes. The purpose of all this rocking and rolling is to assess how the insect keeps its balance while airborne – not so easy with a machine that can move through up to eight rotations per second. Not so easy. But still definitely worth a spin.

Dickinson has found that the Rock-n-Roll rotations are detected by the fly's halteres, or rudimentary hind wings – 'essential elements of the fly's control system,' he explains. 'Cut them off, and [the fly] rapidly corkscrews to the ground.' Once the halteres have sensed the forward, backward or sideward motion, strong wing strokes kick in to oppose it. It's a fast and efficient reflex – rotation leads to detection leads to wing compensation and then stabilisation. Almost instantaneously. That's why staying balanced is pretty easy for the fly. It's as easy as falling off a log – or, in this case, not falling off a log.

MAKING MACHINES THAT FLY LIKE FLIES

Watching a fly fly could be something like watching water boil or paint dry. In other words, endless, pointless and a rather dull thing to do with the waking, working hours of your day. But it's not. In fact, watching a fly fly is a means to a very important end. Especially if you are a fly bioengineer like Michael Dickinson, or one of the other magnificent men making fly-inspired machines.

'So what can we do with this emerging blueprint of a fly?' asks Dickinson. 'Do we know enough to build a robotic insect?' The answer is almost yes. There is a range of current projects at various institutions, but they all share a similar fascination with what differentiates real insect flight from that of the flying machines that already exist.

So what can we do with this emerging blueprint of a fly? Do we know enough to build a robotic insect? The answer is almost yes.

A quick comparison: insects flap their wings, but airplanes don't. It sounds simple, but when it comes to aerodynamic engineering this distinction is quite profound. Planes operate under what's called steady-state aerodynamics – their wings stay still and elevation is achieved by air flowing faster over the top surfaces than the bottom. Insect elevation is not so steady – thanks to all the wing-flapping there is a lot of movement that generates eddies and airpools flowing in the opposite direction to the main current flow. The good news? These eddies help to keep the insects aloft. The bad news? They give scientists a lot more things to think about when designing mini-robotic flies.

A quick comparison: insects flap their wings, but airplanes don't. It sounds simple, but when it comes to aerodynamic engineering this distinction is quite profound.

They have to think about `delayed stall', which happens when the insect's wing sweeps forward at a steep angle that would cause a fixed-wing aircraft to drop and stall. Then there is `rotational circulation', when the wing creates a tennis ball-like backspin that helps the insect achieve more lift. And finally `wake capture', which happens when the wing flaps into its own air-current wake, creating more energy and even more lift.

Clearly, none of these specific flaps and airflows affect the function of fixed-wing planes. So, if you want your mini-robotic fly to behave like its non-robotic counterpart, you have a lot of extra information to integrate. Every natural fly action and eddy has to be studied, understood and then mechanically reproduced. It's a tough job. But there are some big brains doing it.

You would think there were enough flies in the world already. But a number of military and academic teams are still working fervently to build even more ...

THE MICROMECHANICAL FLYING INSECT (MFI) PROJECT

The MFI project started in 1998. The goal of the project – in its designers' own words – is to 'develop a 25 millimetre (wingtip-to-wingtip) device capable of sustained autonomous flight.' A small creation, but still a rather large goal. It's supported by the US Defense Advanced Research Projects Agency (DARPA), although the MFI project's proposed robotic insect will actively flap its wings and be six times smaller than DARPA's 15 centimetre proposed size.

This is where much of the data from Dickinson's Robofly has come in to land. It's a collaboration, a combination of his team's insights into fly flight with the nuts-and-bolts skills of a robotics group from the University of California, Berkeley, led by Professor Ronald Fearing.

Fearing is a professor in the Department of Electrical Engineering and Computer Sciences. He is also director of the Biomimetic Millisystems Lab – a mechanical menagerie where milli-bot birds and insects fly, crawl and scuttle around, and recreated gecko-feet adhesives stick to surfaces and climb the walls. He is a recipient of the 1991 Presidential Young Investigator Award and a co-inventor of 12 US patents. The perfect person to take Dickinson's fly flight theory and bring it to life.

The UCLA Biomimetic Millisystems Lab is a mechanical menagerie where mini-robot birds and insects fly, crawl and scuttle around, and recreated gecko-feet adhesives stick to surfaces and climb the walls.

'It's the mechanical component of this biological system that we, as engineers, are the furthest away from being able to replicate,' writes Dickinson. 'Flies don't have an internal skeleton ... Instead, they are surrounded by an external skeleton – a single continuous sheet composed of proteins, lipids, and the polysaccharide chitin.' The question is, how do you recreate a structure that's not just harder on the

Perhaps one of the most complex skeletal structures known is the wing hinge of an insect – an interconnected tangle of tiny, hard elements embedded in a thinner, more elastic cuticle of rubberlike resilin.

outside than the inside, but also punctuated by lots of complicated soft parts, like folding legs and flexing wing joints?

'Perhaps the most elaborate example of an arthropod joint, indeed one of the most complex skeletal structures known, is the wing hinge of insects,' Dickinson continues. He describes it as an 'interconnected tangle of tiny, hard elements embedded in a thinner, more elastic cuticle of a rubberlike material called resilin, and bordered by the thick side walls of the thorax.' That does sound elaborate. And more elaborate means more difficult to emulate.

Add to this the fact that, in flies, the flight muscles don't actually attach to the hinge they need to flap. Rather, they pull on and strain the thorax walls when they contract. So now the question is: How do you recreate something that's hard on the outside, elastic on the inside and full of complicated soft parts that move in all sorts of complicated ways? The answer is, you ask Ron Fearing.

Through the MFI collaboration, Fearing and team have built a fly wing joint that can flap and rotate much like the real thing. This structure has now found its place in a two-winged, carbon-fibre creature about the size and weight of a large housefly. With nothing more than a few solar-powered batteries, this milli-bot system is able to generate lift. But it's far from taking flight or being finished. Since development, the aim has been to decrease the MFI's weight, while increasing power and enhancing wing control.

Next up will be hovering capabilities and an on-board flight-control and communication system. What use is a robotic fly if you can't make it loiter around the lunch table from afar?

THE ENTOMOPTER

It's either a multimodal electromechanical insect or the Entomopter, depending on your reading material and mood. Most of the time the latter is the name of choice – probably because it sounds as exciting as it is.

> The Entomopter is a two-in-one flyer and crawler. A robotic insect that's designed to flap its wings, creep through ventilation systems and even crawl under doors.

Stemming from the Latin for `insect' (entomo) and `wing' (pteron), the Entomopter is like a super-specialised subspecies of MAV or MFI. It's an ultra-evolved robotic insect that's specifically designed to operate indoors. It's also a two-in-one flyer and crawler – not only can it flap its wings, but it's also destined to creep through ventilation systems and crawl under doors. Which is more than the average natural insect can do. A clear case of creation becoming superior to the inspiration ... or the larva becoming parent to the fly.

In July 2000 Robert Michelson, research engineer at the Georgia Tech Research Institute (GTRI) of the Georgia Institue of Technology, was granted a patent for his invention, the Entomopter. It looks like a toy – a sort of model biplane that a bunch of kids might try unsuccessfully to fly around the park, before losing interest and leaving it on the grass. It's also yellow, a difficult colour to take seriously in scientific circles. But no matter. The Entomopter is really a sophisticated piece of bioinspirational engineering that's holding the interest of an impressive global design team, including GTRI, Cambridge University, and even people from DARPA and NASA. This toy could someday be going to Mars, and to war.

A quick Entomopter physiology lesson: it's powered by a chemical reaction that converts fuel into flapping. This happens in a brilliant, mini-anatomical engine called a Reciprocating Chemical Muscle or RCM. Basically, a chemical fuel is injected into the engine, which

Micro flying things are predicted to find use ubiquitously, from spying on enemies and searching for disaster survivors to assessing chemical spills and measuring emissions in smokestacks.

leads to a reaction that releases a gas. From there it's a simple case of gas pressure building up, pushing on a piston, which pushes on the wings. The energy generated can also be used to power Entomopter sensors and to drive movement for turning, rolling, foot-scurrying and any other future function that might be devised. In short, this RCM is the brawn behind what the Entomopter can do. According to Michelson, the next step would be to shrink the RCM down to be more bug-appropriate -- more or less housefly size.

Yes, the prototype is still more toy-size than tiny, but there are big plans for its future, smaller incarnations. It already has legs, wings and front- and rear-facing sensors. Upcoming versions could also have a radio antenna, camera or even an olfactory sensor for sniffing and tracking odours. These could come in handy. Especially since micro flying things are predicted to find use in nearly everything, from spying on enemies and searching for disaster survivors to assessing chemical spills and measuring emissions in smokestacks. When they aren't going to Mars, that is. (More on that particular Entomopter mission in Chapter 7.)

DRONES

'You probably wouldn't notice a fly in the room, but you certainly would notice a hawk,' says Harvard microbot researcher Professor Robert Wood. Similarly, an enemy of the state probably wouldn't notice a fly-sized microbot in the terrorist cell headquarters, but he would certainly notice a hawk-sized one. This truism was the basis for more than seven years of Wood's work, which culminated in 2007 in a 60-milligram, three cm-wingspan robotic fly – the smallest bot yet to be capable of take-off and sustained flight.

A former PhD student of UCLA biorobotics expert, Ron Fearing, Robert Wood is equally passionate about flies and what makes them fly. 'When I got the fly to take off, I was literally jumping up and down in the lab,' he told Technology Review. But his DARPA-funded micro-spy fly development couldn't have come at a better time. Why? Because things are already starting to change in the way we wage war.

The idea is to have fewer people on the ground and more remote-controlled flying things in the air. Militarily speaking, this is safer, stealthier and potentially more successful – like in 2011 when the CIA scoped out Osama bin Laden's compound in Pakistan using video footage from a bat-winged drone. That's a mission impossible for even the most gung-ho GI. Hence the army's gradual shift from human resources to the not-so-human.

> The idea is to have fewer people on the ground and more remote-controlled flying things in the air. Like in 2011 when the CIA scoped out Osama bin Laden's compound in Pakistan using video footage from a bat-winged drone.

A decade ago the Pentagon had about 50 aerial drones on staff. Now it has over 7,000, and more remote pilots in training than it has fighter and bomber pilots combined. Large and mid-range drones with intimidating names like the Global Hawk, the Predator, the Reaper and the Shadow have already made remote-controlled international missions powered by joysticks and computers on US military-base soil. But smaller is still better. The plan is to channel something like $5 billion a year into drone development, with spy-flies taking flight by 2030, complete with mod-cons like microcameras and sensors for detecting anything from nuclear weapons and bad-guys-in-hiding, to good-guy survivors stuck or lost behind enemy lines.

Some of the smaller bird- and moth-inspired bots are being developed at the Wright-Patterson Air Force Base in Ohio, in an aptly named building called the Microaviary. Then there is Robert Wood's microfly, which might be the tiniest drone developed yet.

At just three centimetre wingtip to wingtip, it's a stealth soldier in the making. But its unparalleled petiteness is also its biggest problem. Wood and team couldn't use readymade nuts, bolts, motors and manufacturing processes to make their super-special-tiny-mini-drone. They also couldn't just scale down what already existed – they needed ultra-efficient but featherweight parts that were capable of going through the complicated motions of fly flight. They have also had to consider things like an on-board power source, sensors and obstacle-avoidance software – all within the 60-milligram weight limit. Clearly drones have baggage restrictions, too.

THE FLIGHT AHEAD

Aerodynamic engineers aren't that interested in bumblebees – except when they are trying to prove that the poor things shouldn't be able to fly at all. This is the equivalent of a mathematical fat joke and, sadly for the rotund bumblers, it makes quite a lot of sense.

We have all seen it. The flight of the bumblebee is a graceless, helter-skelter process that has inspired not much more than an equally helter-skelter piece of classical music with the same name. The flight of the fly, on the other hand, has inspired the development of a swarm of agile, airborne mini-mercenaries. No one's saying that one is better than the other. But you can certainly judge a creature by what it moves the human mind to do.

When it comes to bio-inspiration, flies are clearly big contributors to inventions for flight. It is all in the name. We have got the best bio-inspirer on the job.

We can't help it, really. We humans are natural copycats (we have even copied cats – like their eyes, which we have mimicked to mark our roads at night). But, when it comes to bioinspiration, flies are clearly big contributors to inventions for flight. It's all in the name. We have got the best bioinspirer on the job.

The amount of time, money and cool gadgetry that's been devoted to studying flies says a great deal about how much the insect's flight skills deserve our respect. But it's not just their wings – scientists are fascinated by the fly's entire anatomical aviation system, including the nerves, brain, legs, thorax and eyes. They may not fully understand the systems they study, but that doesn't mean they can't use what they learn.

'We can build a system that works perfectly well, inspired by biology, without having a complete understanding of how the components interact,' computational neuroscientist Professor David O'Carroll told Wired magazine. O'Carroll is an insect-vision enthusiast with a lab in the Department of Physiology at the University of Adelaide in Australia. Here, a team has meticulously measured the cell-by-cell activity in the fly's optical flight circuit and turned it into a set of mathematical equations that could be used in future MFIs' optical circuits.

'We started with insect vision as an inspiration, and built a model that's feasible for real-world use,' says O'Carroll. 'But in doing so, we have built a system almost as complicated as the insect's. That's one of the fascinating things here,' he continues. 'It doesn't necessarily lead us to a complete understanding of how the system works, but to an appreciation that nature got it right.'

The plan is to channel something like $5 billion a year into drone development, with spy-flies taking flight by 2030.

Nature always gets it right, and even our best inventions have to run to keep up. Or fly to keep up, depending on the invention and the day.

If we had fly eyes to help us see further ahead, we would probably be able to tell exactly when MFIs will officially start revolutionising human flight. But we can't. We're only human. All we can do is keep trying to develop the best tiny, unmanned flying machines we can, in the hope that one day they will function like the real thing.

CHAPTER 7

FLY IN SPACE

WHAT DO DOGS, chimpanzees, mice and spiders have in common with rye seeds, cotton seeds, moss, newts, chicken embryos and frogs? Here's a clue: It's something they all have in common with flies.

Here's another clue: It has nothing to do with witches, cauldrons or hubbling, bubbling, toiling and troubling (a logical assumption whenever there are frogs and newts involved). All the same, there is nothing sinister or Shakespearean about this diverse list of animals and plants. It's simple, really. They have all been into space.

At one time or another, each of these organisms has been placed in a sealed metal capsule, launched off the Earth's surface with much ceremony and pomp, and then powered through the atmosphere on a tail of flaming rocket fuel. But, of these space-faring species, the fly should probably be mentioned first. Why? Because it made the journey first – along with the rye and cotton seeds. But hey were passive passengers, so we will focus on the astronautical fauna and let the flora lie.

It was 1947. The US was thinking about sending a man into space. Thinking about it a lot, in fact. When they weren't thinking about it, they were worrying about it – about the possible radiation in space, how it might affect a human and whether it could be prevented with some sort of fancy protective shield. They decided to do some research into radiation at high altitudes to see if it really was worth worrying about. That's when the US military launched a rocket into the edge of space. On board were some fruit flies. The Yuri Gagarins of the animal world.

In 1947 the US military launched a rocket into the edge of space. On board were some fruit flies. The first organisms in space. The Yuri Gagarins of the animal world.

It's not surprising that the fruit fly was chosen. Again. *Drosophila* (often called the `golden bug' in scientific circles) is a natural choice when researchers want to test how something will affect human DNA, because humans and fruit flies share a number of genes and therefore a tendency to be similarly affected by DNA-mutating factors. Like radiation, which could be a factor in space.

Fortunately, on this mission it wasn't. The flies were up and down in no time and alive to fly again. As they so often are after a brush with death – much to the frustration of the person wielding the brush. From rapid rise to gentle descent by parachute, the whole mission took just over three minutes. The flies made it back, not just intact, but also genetically unmutated. Confirmed: high-altitude radiation should not be a spanner in the space programme's works. At ease everyone. Back to the business of thinking about sending men into space.

FLIES FLYING HIGHER

A colony of fruit flies was on-board *Atlantis*, the last craft to return to Earth in NASA's 30-year Space Shuttle Program.

It was a quick pop-up for a few flies, but a giant journey for animals of all kinds. In 1948, monkeys survived a ride beyond the atmosphere. By 1957 a dog made it all the way into orbit. Then, in 1961, Russia launched the first true spaceman – the real Yuri Gagarin who became a hero of the Soviet Union and a global celebrity in the time it takes to circle the Earth, watch the average romantic comedy or play a football game to time. About 90 minutes in the case of all three.

Since then, fruit flies have continued to be recruited for regular research missions into space. Even 60 years later, on the last space shuttle mission of them all.

It was 2011. July. The stragglers were coming home to roost after NASA's 30-year Space Shuttle Program was finally declared over and out. Last one in was *Atlantis*, carrying various bits and pieces from the International Space Station, including two golden orb spiders called Gladys and Esmerelda.

The pair of oddly named arachnids had just spent a couple of months in space growing and spinning webs so scientists could assess the effects of microgravity on their behaviour. A colony of fruit flies was on-board too – no names for these guys, probably because one of their chief jobs on this mission was to be spider food for the Golden Orb Girls. This meant that many of the flies didn't survive to fulfil their other job, namely to move and fly around so that scientists could assess how low-gravity affected them too. But some did, returning to Earth to join a long line of flies who have contributed as much to space travel as they have to science.

Why are flies such regular space racers? Mostly because they are fast-breeding, low-maintenance travellers, meaning even short space missions end up carrying multiple generations of flies. Plus their DNA is similar to ours, but mutates quicker to allow for speedier and more convenient study. One much publicised NASA-sanctioned experiment in 2006 studied the fruit fly immune system in space – and, by implication, the similar, albeit more complex, human immune system in space.

'The fruit fly life cycle is quicker,' NASA researcher Sharmila Bhattacharya told InterSpace News at the time, 'so we can study an animal that develops most of its life in space.' In fact, the mission time spanned more than a third of *Drosophila*'s lifecycle. It was only a 13-day journey. But the 100 fruit fly eggs that took off had hatched into larvae before arriving at the International Space Station. Once there, they set about eating, growing, maturing and multiplying to make the 10 cd-sized Plexiglas containers they were travelling in even more cramped. The flies were fed only once – a single helping of a gelatin-sugar mixture – on the whole mission. Less even than in cattle-class on a budget airline. Still, several thousand flies made the journey home. Too many members of the Mile High Club to count.

It was a 13-day journey and the flies were fed only once. A single helping of a gelatin-sugar mixture.

The assumption was that the 'stressful situation they were in would affect the immune system,' said Bhattacharya. 'We are looking at changes after a long time in space, to see if [the flies] have increased levels of proteins to fight infections.' Therefore, once back on Earth, the spaceflies' food was sprinkled with an infective fungus called *Beauveria bassiana,* which made the same trip on the same shuttle. Their immune response to the infection was compared to that of a control group of flies that never left NASA's Kennedy Space Center in Florida. The idea is to use the results to help humans stay safer and healthier in space – as well as to work out how prolonged low-gravity places the body and all its systems under strain.

This is how flies are helping humans to travel further, and safer. Various short-term shuttle projects suggest that the immune system is not a major concern on minor space missions. But two weeks at low- to no-gravity is small change compared to the physical and mental price that the body pays for a more extended stay.

There is still much to learn before humans can safely set off for two- or three-year interplanetary trips. And which creature do you think will be called in to help?

'Every time you fly in space you are an experiment,' Dr Scott Parazynski told CNN in a 2006 interview. Fruit flies certainly know that feeling. A physician and NASA astronaut, Parazynski has been just such an experiment on four shuttle missions. He explains that, although there is some data on longer space journeys – for instance Russian cosmonaut Valeri Poliakov's 438-day stay at the MIR space station – there is still much to learn before humans can safely set off for two- or three-year interplanetary trips. And which creature do you think will be called in to help? Here's a clue: It's not a spider or a newt.

Even in our post-Space Shuttle Program age this is knowledge worth having. Perhaps more so now than ever before. Why? Because future space races are likely to involve longer distances and therefore even longer-haul flights.

Not quite to infinity or beyond. But, at the very least, to Mars.

FLIES FLYING FURTHER

The first person who takes a step on Mars could also end up being the first person with a broken leg on Mars. This would certainly put a damper on things and ruin the made-for-TV moment.

According to NASA, this is all gravity's fault. Before the leg even extends itself to take that first historic step, it will experience a range of gravitational flick-flacks that could set it up for a fall. First it has to exit Earth's familiar gravitational pull and experience several Gs (or Earthly gravitational forces) while launching. Then it will cruise to the Red Planet – a three-month trip at just about zero-gravity – followed by a several-G landing on the Martian surface and then a planetary gravitational pull that's a mere 38 percent of that on Earth. This is called microgravity. And, whether it's zero-G or a fraction of a G, it's not so good for bodies (and legs) that are adapted to living in a macrogravity environment.

> The higher we want to fly and the further we want to go into space, the more deeply we need to understand the effects of gravity and the closer we need to look at fruit flies.

Gravitational forces are known to affect various body parts in different ways. According to a multicentre study on the effects of long-duration spaceflight published in 2010 in the Journal of Cosmology, crew members on 4 to twelve month missions 'have experienced losses in bone mineral density and bone strength, decreased muscle volume and peak muscle power, expansion of intervertebral discs, and alterations in balance and other sensorimotor functions'.

The result is a combination of weak muscles, weak bones and weak balance. Which of course leads to a stronger chance of fracturing a bone when you take even one small step onto microgravity ground.

Then there are gravity's more subtle effects – like changes in gene expression, the process by which the information from a gene is used in action, for example, in the synthesis of a gene product like a cell. Evidently, the higher we want to fly and the further we want to go into space, the more deeply we need to understand the effects of gravity and the closer we need to look at fruit flies.

Fruit flies move more in space, but they also age more quickly – after extended time in microgravity conditions, adult male flies die earlier on return to Earth.

The library of space-related fruit fly research is well-stocked -- if not well-thumbed by anyone who isn't a cosmonaut or aeronautically inclined. Past studies show that, in general, *Drosophila* flies become more mobile in space. Not only do they move more, they also age more quickly – after extended time in microgravity conditions, adult male flies die earlier on return to Earth. That's interesting. Even more interesting, when scientists simulate low-gravity on the ground, fruit fly subjects have been found to undergo similar changes to those in space, but the changes are less pronounced. This means that, when it comes to space-travel physiology, there is more than just gravity to consider. For humans and for flies.

For instance, consider the 2003 GENE experiment, which sent a batch of fruit flies to the International Space Station for gene-expression analysis. It was found that the pupaenauts showed far more gene-expression changes than controls who stayed home in a microgravity simulation system. In other words, gravity does affect gene expression, but so do space-flight stresses like temperature swings and reduced gaseous exchange.

Clearly, there is something about space that messes with multiple systems. Something that can't be simulated on the ground. And once again the golden bug has shed some light on a growing list of risk factors for human bodies headed for further-flung space. Gravity. Temperature. Gaseous exchange. Altered ageing and genetic expression. All things worth factoring in on a possible mission to Mars. But what about getting there, and getting around once you have arrived? Also worth factoring in? In fact, why bother tackling the above factors if you don't even have a form of transport for the trip? Turns out the fly might have a hand in that too. Or rather a wing or two.

FLYING LESSONS FROM FLIES

Think back to Chapter 6 and the Entomopter – the patented flying machine with wings that really flap – an insect-inspired flying and crawling device that's set to become a tiny, unmanned micro-air vehicle (MAV) for mostly military use. That's if it's downscaled from a current wingspan of 15 centimetre to intended housefly-size. But it could also possibly be upscaled. To a one metre wingspan and future spacecraft status on Mars.

'The first serious look at flying on Mars was done in the mid-1970s,' wrote Entomopter inventor and developer Professor Robert Michelson in a paper for the 2010 International Unmanned Vehicles Workshop. 'Since then there have been numerous studies and designs ... Because of the very low atmospheric density on Mars all of these conventional aircraft designs have come across the same limitation, in order to generate sufficient lift the aircraft must fly fast.'

Very, very fast. At least as fast as 350 kilometres per hour to avoid stalling, in fact. But this need for speed is not the only problem. So is the rockiness of the Red Planet's surface – a problem, says Michelson, that 'makes it almost impossible to produce a conventional aircraft that can safely land and take off again'. As a result, all previously proposed missions have been limited in duration by the amount of fuel the craft could carry for a single flight.

Very low atmospheric density on Mars means that, in order to generate sufficient lift, an aircraft must fly as fast as 350 kilometres per hour.

Yet another challenge. Landing is a problem, but so is generating lift.

'Mars is a nasty place to fly a conventional air vehicle because almost everything there is working against you,' says Anthony Colozza, principal investigator for the Ohio Aerospace Institute (OAI) and coordinator of the Entomopter study. Some of the nasty forces at work include extreme temperature swings that mess with materials and fuels, as well as a wafer-thin atmosphere that's 95 percent carbon dioxide and only one-tenth of a percent oxygen.

High CO_2 levels mean propellers can't spin as fast as on Earth without creating destructive shock waves. The CO_2 atmosphere lowers the speed of sound by 20 percent, which further limits aircraft and propeller speed. The lower-than normal O_2 on the other hand, is asphyxiating for oxygen-hungry engines. Not a nice set-up for any conventionally powered craft.

> The Entomopter is a fly-inspired craft that would use the same lift-generating mechanisms that insects do on Earth to get around on the rocky Red Planet.

'The Entomopter concept is really a breath of fresh air because it makes the environment of Mars our friend,' says Colozza. The unconventional design does not try to fit in with the challenges of the Martian environment. It doesn't try to be a superfast, fuel-lugging, non-landing flying machine. It just is what it is: a fly-inspired flier that happens to use the same lift-generating mechanisms that insects do on Earth, to get around on the rocky Red Planet. It's a happy coincidence. A match made on Mars.

'Fixed-wing vehicles must fly too fast in the thin Mars atmosphere to avoid stall,' writes Michelson. So, in addition to speeding past areas of scientific interest, they can't even land to refuel or take a closer look. But, while fixed-wing craft are forced to move at high speeds and in one piece to generate lift, Entomopters (like the insects that inspire them) can flap their wings at superhigh speeds – while their bodies move slowly enough to fully appreciate the details of the Martian landscape (or manure pile) they are flying over and exploring.

The happy coincidences continue. Here are three more. Firstly, gravity on Mars is only 38 percent of Earth's. This means the Entomopter could be easily augmented to aircraft size without the proportional weight-gain it would experience on Earth. Secondly, the planet's low-oxygen atmosphere is no problem for the Entomopter's Reciprocating Chemical Muscle power source – it feeds the device's flapping and functioning with a variety of fuels, none of which is O_2 gas. Thirdly, 'flapping wings are more survivable and robust in the presence of foreign object damage,' says Michelson. This is a scientific way of saying they are better at being bashed around. 'It is a well-documented fact,' he continues, 'that birds and insects are able to sustain collisions with walls (or one another) without major damage when they become trapped indoors. Rotors and propellers, on the other hand, concentrate all of their energy at their rotational frequency and tend to explode when coming into contact with objects.'

Entomopters (like the insects that inspire them) can flap their wings at super-high speeds, while their bodies move slowly enough to fully appreciate the details of the Martian landscape (or manure pile) they are flying over and exploring.

Stronger. Slower. More fuel-savvy. It's no wonder the Entomopter is so perfectly poised for greener pastures with redder horizons. Even now, more than 10 years after the initial patent, research into a bigger, better, more Mars-bound version continues. It's an ongoing, multicentre, biomimicry programme that includes scientists like Michelson and Colozza, and various others at the University of Missouri-Rolla, Ohio Aerospace Institute and, needless to say, NASA.

Potential hopes and dreams include a fleet (or flock, or swarm) of multimode Entomopters flying and crawling across the surface of Mars. They could work from an altitude of about 30 metres, gathering photos and videos and sampling all sorts of substances from the ground and the air. They could use a remote-controlled rover vehicle as a base for take-off, landings, data-downloads and refuels. They could guide the rover to the most interesting spots for study and then fly over canyons and boulders that the landlubber couldn't traverse.

Let's face it. Space is not very hospitable to humans. And Mars in particular is nasty to people and planes alike. But, still, we can't stop trying to get there. So we will take any help we can get.

Flies made it into space before we did. They will probably beat us to Mars too. Then, when we finally get there, it will probably be because a fly has proved that it's safe – and then inspired the development of just the right machine to make the trip. Frogs and newts are all very well. But when it comes to space travel, the magic ingredient is still the fly.

CHAPTER 8

FLY AT THE CRIME SCENE

THERE IS A FIELD IN NORMAN, OKLAHOMA, that is sometimes dotted with the bodies of dead pigs in clothes.

Some of them are fully clothed – little trotters poking out of rumpled shirts, or shorts stretched tight over plump piggy thighs. Others are completely naked, just skin and muscle and bone rotting in the grass. There are small dead pigs and big dead pigs. Babies and kids and parents all scattered around like the aftermath of a pig genocide or plague. There are small T-shirts and bigger T-shirts, twisted around dead and decaying shapes. There are things crawling in the creases. And there are students with face masks, test tubes and magnifying glasses crawling between the bodies to take a closer look.

It's a game of academic Cluedo, a field trip for an Oklahoma University course called 'Bones and Bugs: An Introduction to Forensic Archaeology and Forensic Entomology'. Dr Heather Ketchum, assistant professor in the university's Department of Zoology, sets up the porcine crime scenes in advance. Then the students arrive to collect evidence, assess the level of putrefaction and insect invasion and work out whether it was it Colonel Mustard in the ballroom with the candlestick or Farmer Brown in the abattoir with a knife.

That's what forensic entomologists do. They use their knowledge of insect biology to piece together the story of a death. The detailed story. The gory story. Complete with how it happened, when it happened, who did it and who's trying to cover it up.

It's no coincidence that the band of US entomologists who pioneered the forensic field in the 1980s called themselves the Dirty Dozen. If you want to know dirty little secrets, you have to spend time with dirty little things that are

The US entomologists who pioneered the forensic field in the 1980s called themselves the Dirty Dozen. If you want to know dirty little secrets, you have to spend time with dirty little things that are drawn to death and decay.

drawn to decay. Things like beetles, mites, moths, ants, bees, wasps and flies – all kinds of flies from blowflies and houseflies to flesh flies, cheese flies, coffin flies, black soldier flies, humpbacked flies, sun flies, lesser corpse flies and black scavenger flies. The names say it all.

Clearly, flies are very important in this field – the Norman, Oklahoma field and the field of forensic entomology itself. Each fly's particular time of arrival and tastes give the entomologists clues as to when death occurred and the buffet opened for business.

Blowflies can smell death from up to 16 kilometres away. They got their name from the fact that, when they lay their eggs in meat, it gets blown up or `fly blown'.

Blowflies got their name from the fact that, when they lay their eggs in meat, it gets blown up or `fly blown'. They can smell death from up to 16 kilometres away, which is why these flies are often the first insects to find their way onto a corpse and therefore into a forensic report. Flesh flies are named for their love of rotting flesh. They love it so much that they aren't fussy about how long it's been decomposing – as long as it's dead, they will land on it and lay their young. Cheese flies, on the other hand, are usually latecomers to a corpse, appearing only three to six months after death. They might have been named for a penchant for cheese, but they also enjoy cured meat, smoked fish and decaying flesh. Because they can delay dining on the latter for so long, they can be useful in cases involving older corpses.

Some might consider entomology a dirty job. But forensic entomology is dirtier by far. It's the underbelly of insect-study. In addition to lots of bugs, it calls for lots of dead bodies. And, evidently, lots of pigs.

'I once put a 50-pound dead pig wrapped in blankets in my backyard to decompose to mimic a body in a homicide case,' said Dr Lee Goff in an interview with National Geographic News. 'We were trying to determine how long it takes insects to penetrate the wrapping,' he explains. How do you explain that to your neighbours?

Goff is director of the Forensic Sciences programme at Chaminade University in Honolulu, Hawaii. He is also a consultant on various television crime investigation dramas, including the eponymous *CSI: Crime Scene Investigation*. But he wasn't always doing high-profile interviews and contributing case studies for TV. It's been a career metamorphosis as fascinating as a fly's. Goff hatched as a regular entomologist, went through a forensic larval phase as one of the original Dirty Dozen and pupated as a frequent expert witness and author of the book *A Fly for the Prosecution*. He finally flew to fame when several of the case studies in his book became *CSI* episode scripts. He still teaches, researches and investigates crime scenes, to which he usually arrives on a Harley-Davidson.

'I once put a 50-pound dead pig wrapped in blankets in my backyard to decompose to mimic a body in a homicide case'. — Dr Lee Goff, forensic entomologist

'A 50-pound pig most closely represents human decomposition,' he says. 'It's the next best thing to a human corpse. We have a secure area in part of the university and in various military zones where we can let the animals decompose. We also put [them] in a range of different environments – in rain forests, arid volcanic craters, tidal pools – to see how conditions change the rate of decomposition. We have hung pigs in trees to see how decay differs ... We have buried them and burnt them to varying degrees to see the effects.'

Ballroom or abattoir, Colonel Mustard or Farmer Brown, volcanic crater or fetid rockpool, forensic entomology uses lots of pigs and flies to reveal the truth. Probably more maggots than flies – but that all depends on the time since death.

EXPERT, INSECT WITNESS

Flies were helping to solve crimes long before forensic entomology was even a twinkle in a scientist's eye. The first recorded case was in 1235 in a small village in China. A man was found slashed up by a hand sickle in the hand of an unknown fellow farm worker and peasant. But the magistrate – clearly a forensically and entomologically minded man – knew that his most powerful weapon would be the murder weapon itself. So he called all village suspects and their hand sickles into the town square. Set down your tools and step back, the men were instructed. Which they did. And everyone watched.

The day was warm so it didn't take long. The flies arrived to loop and buzz around the square – as they always do when heat is rising, people are gathering and traces of human tissue lie baking on a metal blade in the sun. That's what the flies made a beeline for. The single sickle of the 10 that still bore the victim's blood.

'The witnesses of the murder were the brightly metallic-coloured flies known as the blowflies which had been attracted to the remaining bits of soft tissue, blood, bone and hair'. — Sung Tz'u, 13th-century forensic medical expert

'Within just a few minutes many had landed on the hand sickle and were crawling over it with interest,' wrote forensic medical expert Sung Tz'u in his 1247 book, *The Washing Away of Wrongs*. 'None of the other hand sickles had attracted any of these pretty flies. The owner of the tool became very nervous, and it was only a few more moments before all those in the village knew who the murderer was.'

It's like an ancient Chinese Sherlock Holmes story. The magistrate is Holmes and Sung Tz'u the Sir Arthur Conan Doyle who immortalised him. 'The witnesses of the murder were the brightly metallic-coloured flies known as the blowflies which had been attracted to the remaining bits of soft tissue, blood, bone and hair which had stuck to the hand sickle after the murder was committed,' wrote Tz'u. 'The knowledge of the village magistrate as to a specific insect group's behaviour regarding their attraction to dead human tissue was the key to solving this violent act and justice was served.'

Not so elementary, especially for the time. But so the story of forensic entomology had begun, with the blowfly already its dramatic lead.

It took a while for the facts to rise to the top of the fiction. Only in 1668 did someone work out that maggots don't automatically sprout from the rotting meat in which they are found – an accepted theory of the day called spontaneous generation. That someone was Italian physician Francesco Redi, whose experiments showed that larvae couldn't or wouldn't appear in meat that was not exposed to air. Therefore, they had to have come from without, not within, their favourite food. It was a confusing contradiction of everything that had come before.

In 1668 an Italian physician worked out that maggots don't automatically sprout from the rotting meat in which they are found – an accepted theory of the day called spontaneous generation.

Further investigation into decay and fly development ensued. The field of forensic entomology was growing into a more scientifically sound version of itself. More than 500 years later, it still is. Mostly because it's not enough simply to know that flies and larvae are naturally drawn to fetid flesh. Of course we know that. We are reminded of it every time we cross paths with a restaurant rubbish bin or smudge of roadkill. But the more we know about this insect's natural interaction with all things foul, the more it whispers sweet testimonies in our ears.

Yes, the fly is the ultimate eyewitness. Not just for murder, but also for suicide, physical neglect, abuse and most other forms of foul play that continue to plague us. Here's what its whispers can show ...

WHEN DID IT HAPPEN?

This is the bread and butter of the forensic entomologist's job. The postmortem interval (PMI), Time Since Colonisation, or in lay terms, the time since death. In the sandwich of facts that the investigation can reveal, this is generally first on the plate and the simplest bit to prepare. Why? Because if you are an entomologist, you will know insect life cycles by heart. You will know the order in which waves of insects arrive to colonise a carcas, known as faunal succession. You will know their ages and stages of development by sight. You will know which parts of the body they best like to eat and in which crooks and crevices they prefer to lay their eggs.

In this way, insect infestation tracks death in terms of time. It's like a Swiss stopwatch, and, because they have been so closely studied, blowflies are its most reliable part. They arrive early. The early blow-flies catch more than the worms. The first on the scene appear within minutes if the weather is warm and the body isn't left lying in a closed room. It's thought that they use chemical signals to attract followers from kilometres away. In just a few hours, there is a blowfly carnival. Fleets of flyers feed into crowds of crawlers, the females laying globules of eggs around wet wounds and every exposed orifice they can find.

They like to work as a team, becoming a maggot mass – a packed, churning mob that feeds voraciously enough to generate up to 53°C of heat. Enough heat to scald the skin of the body if it was still alive.

Twelve to 72 hours later there are throngs of tiny blowfly larvae eating, hooking, tearing and secreting enzymes into the tissue around them. They grow in number and size over days or weeks. They like to work as a team, becoming a maggot mass – a packed, churning mob that feeds voraciously enough to generate up to 53°C of heat. Enough heat to scald the skin of the body if it was still alive. Enough heat to force the maggots in the centre of the mass to make a desperate crawl for the outskirts in search of relief. Once they have fed themselves up to third-instar phase, the plump larvae leave in search of dry, dark soil or inviting folds of clothing or bedding for pupation. The adult flies that later emerge may or may not return to the body. The cycle continues and the corpse becomes a hot mess. A disintegrating, dissolving, liquefying mess.

The heat from the maggot mass certainly helps the process of decay. So does the frenzied hooking, eating and secreting. Because they can increase their own body weight by several hundred times in just a few days, it's been found that feeding larvae can rapidly reduce a corpse's body weight by as much as 60 percent. They can dissolve it down to not much more than bones. The forensic entomologist has to take all of this into account when telling the time of death on a trusty faunal clock.

Because they can increase their own body weight by several hundred times in just a few days, feeding larvae can rapidly reduce the corpse's body weight by as much as 60 percent. They can dissolve it down to not much more than bones.

Blowfly development, in particular, tells very precise postmortem time. In fact, once the blowflies have flown the corpse, it can be quite difficult for an investigator to gauge a time of death. But there can be more difficult things to gauge – like where and how the death went down. This requires an even deeper understanding of insect behaviour. And maybe a couple more experimental pigs.

WHERE AND HOW DID IT HAPPEN?

In 1995, a graduate student at Simon Fraser University (SFU) in Canada sent out an email appeal for used underwear. Yes, used underwear. The newspapers picked up on it. It resulted in a bit of a storm in a bra-cup. But it turned out the underwear was an academic tool. Another forensic entomologist dressing up dead pigs.

'SFU biologist Gail Anderson, a forensic entomologist, is looking for old underwear to complete the outfits she and two graduate students will use to dress pig carcasses,' a university media release explained at the time. '[Anderson] recently discovered that clothing not only affects the body (which 'bloats' after death) but could impact the behaviour of bugs.'

Blowfly maggots prefer their carrion clothed – they will skip over the skin of a naked body because fabric helps to keep flesh moist and therefore more attractive as a meal.

It all worked out in the end. Scandal was averted and science was served. Anderson's underwear-wearing pigs helped show that blowfly maggots prefer their carrion clothed – they will skip over the skin of a naked body because fabric helps to keep flesh moist and therefore more attractive as a meal.

This is worth considering in human cases where clothing is added, changed or removed after death – flies could have tucked in sooner or later than otherwise expected. But there are other how and where factors to consider too. Like whether the death occurred indoors (where infestation takes longer) or outdoors (where it happens faster and more fervently). Or was the corpse moved from one location to another? Was it transported in a car trunk and then dumped? Was it wrapped in garbage bags, newspapers, a tablecloth or a blanket?

You may recall that forensic entomologist Lee Goff wrapped and duct-taped a pig in blankets to solve a murder involving a woman's corpse bound in the same way. It was a difficult case. When the body was found on a Honolulu hillside, the hairy blowfly larvae and unemerged pupae present pointed to 10.5 days of insect activity, and so probably 10.5 days since death. But the arithmetic was off – the wife and her estranged husband (the primary suspect) were heard having a violent fight 13 days before the find. A clear problem for prosecution, until Goff's backyard pig test showed that it took 2.5 days for flies to ferret through the double layer of blanket to the pig body inside. This added up better: 2.5 days of ferreting plus 10.5 days of fly activity equalled 13 days since death. It also equalled a more likely guilty husband. It was a trial by fly. Hairy blowfly, to be precise.

It's not the only case of its kind. Clearly many locations and conditions can complicate the telling of time and place by fly. But they all help entomologist to piece together the foul play that unfolded. Some flies are endemic to certain environments or locales. They can hitch a ride on a dead body and so give clues as to where the murder took place – if typically farm-dwelling maggots are found on a body lying dead in a ballroom, it's safe to start shifting focus from Colonel Mustard to Farmer Brown.

Some flies prefer certain seasons or times of day. Some prefer certain conditions – wet rather than dry, dark rather than light, warm rather than cold. Temperature is a big one. Particularly because larval development is a temperature-dependent process. This means a forensic entomologist will need to consider the weather reports and climate data to see if heat or cold could have affected the flies' breeding and behaviour. Unless, of course, there are no flies on the body at all. Or any other insects for that matter, which suggests something else entirely.

Larval development is a temperature-dependent process. This means a forensic entomologist needs to consider weather reports and climate data to see if heat or cold could have affected the flies' breeding and behaviour.

An eerie, empty corpse found long dead, but all too clean of arthropods, suggests one of three things: the body was buried deep, sealed tight or frozen solid after death. Flies really are the ultimate eyewitnesses. Even their absence tells tales about the events surrounding a death. Sometimes, they leave behind tracks after walking through spilled blood. Or they eat the blood, partially digest it and pass it as so-called flyspecks. If they don't regurgitate it somewhere else and leave blood-spatter analysts scratching their heads.

In the end, flies probably do more forensic good than harm. They might make a mess of things and sometimes complicate the scene of the crime. But they also help clarify and solve it. You just have to read the signs correctly.

WHO WAS TAKING WHAT?

Crime and drugs go together like flies and blood. The one follows the other and gets bigger and stronger as a result. Flies thrive on blood. Crime thrives alongside drugs. It's an unfortunate fact, but one that crime-investigators can use to their advantage.

Let's say a drug-related murder is committed and a body is found. But it's found quite late – late enough for maggots to have stripped it down to dry bones and not much else. This is a problem for drug testing – there is nothing left to test.

The newish field of entomotoxicology rests on the fact that, when larvae eat human flesh they take in any toxins consumed by that human before death. Meaning you can test the tissue of the larvae for drugs.

'In one case I had to determine whether an individual had consumed cocaine before death,' forensic entomologist Lee Goff said in an interview with National Geographic News. 'I wondered whether I could use the maggots, beetles, and pupae that had inhabited the body and test them for drugs. The answer turned out to be yes.'

Lucky for Goff (and for murder victims everywhere) the pharmacological truth will out – even without any soft tissue or fluids like blood or urine that are usually needed for ordinary drug tests. It's a newish field called entomotoxicology, and it rests on the fact that, when larvae eat human flesh, they take in any toxins consumed by that person before death. This means you can test the larvae tissue for the toxin – a convenient development, as drug use and drug-related homicide continue to rise. But it's not so convenient for the bugs who feed on the rising number of bodies.

'A maggot feeding on a long-term heroin addict will actually have a slower growth rate compared with a maggot that is found in a new user, or someone who died of an overdose,' says Goff. A cocaine-user's flesh, on the other hand, will speed things up so the maggots grow more quickly. 'Cocaine, heroin, ecstasy, angel dust [PCP], and amphetamines all affect a bug's life,' says Goff. And as such they tell us even more about the drug-user's death.

'A maggot feeding on a long-term heroin addict will have a slower growth rate compared with a maggot that is found in a new user, or someone who died of an overdose'.
— Dr Lee Goff, forensic entomologist

WHO DID WHAT TO WHOM?

It seems forensic entomologists are a strange bunch. When they are not poring over pupae, they are riding Harley-Davidsons or playing dress-up with pigs. And Mark Benecke is no different. Until 2000 this German forensic scientist spent some of his non-pupa time playing in the punk band, Die Blonden Burschen (The Blonde Boys). Since 2001 he has spent it running the German chapter of the non-governmental organisation, the Transylvanian Society of Dracula (TSD). This is not a joke. But neither are the cases that Benecke works on.

He has been involved in identifying the skull and teeth belonging to Adolf Hitler and Eva Braun. He consults, teaches and acts as an expert witness. Just like any normal forensic entomologist – if there is really such a thing. But Benecke doesn't work exclusively on murder cases. He has written a great deal about the use of forensic entomology in situations involving neglect and abuse – particularly of children and elderly people in nursing homes.

> The green bottle fly can help prove cases of neglect or abuse. It likes the smell of ammonia, which attracts it conspicuously to an incontinent baby or elderly person who isn't changed or washed regularly enough.

In one such case, which he described in a 2001 issue of Forensic Science International, a child was found dead after social workers had repeatedly been called in and reported no evidence of neglect in the home. But the flies said otherwise. In particular the little housefly and the false stable fly – two very telling species found on the genital area of the corpse. Both of these flies are drawn to faeces and urine as opposed to rotting flesh. Evidence of neglect, but unfortunately after the fact. This led to the conclusion that proper legal action against the caregiver – or lack-of-caregiver – could have saved the poor child. The result? The mother went to prison. The social workers were charged with a violation of the duty of care.

It's a fact: different flies like different foods. And forensic entomologists know which ones like what. For example, the green bottle fly likes the smell of ammonia, which attracts it conspicuously to an incontinent baby or elderly person who isn't changed or washed regularly enough. If this neglect persists, the fly might lay eggs, which might then hatch into maggots that will feed on any open wounds or orifices. If the neglect persists, infection can come next. Or even worse, death.

At any point in this process, the flies could be used as evidence of abuse. We can only hope they are found early enough. If not, forensic entomologists could shortly be searching for other fly species to piece together a postmortem interval and facts for a prosecutor's case.

Of course, proving abuse and preventing death is the ideal ending to this episode of *CSI*. But catching the killer through clues on the corpse is a pretty satisfying concluding scene too. Either way, if the right people are paying attention, justice can be served on the wings of a fly. Like clockwork. The natural clockwork of the insect's every move.

CHAPTER 9

FLY FOR FUN

SPIDERS ARE THE SERIOUS ONES. Scorpions are scary, so are bees. Dragonflies and butterflies are pretty, dung beetles industrious, ladybugs are cute. Ants are the arbitrary ones – the constantly moving crowd scenes, the extras on the set of the insect world. Then there are flies. The funny ones. The funniest insects of them all.

They can't help it, really. They are like cartoon characters. Or Jim Carrey. They have big, goggly eyes, six scrawny legs and a habit of flying into things – like traps, windows, cups of coffee and carnivorous plants – and getting themselves killed. Comedy is built into their bodies and comes out in everything they do. Except when they are making people ill. That's not funny at all.

> Flies are built for comedy. They are like cartoon characters. Or Jim Carrey. They have big, goggly eyes, six scrawny legs and a habit of flying into things — and getting themselves killed.

But let's not think about flies' general propensity for death, disease and dung heaps. That's far too serious, and serious matters are better left to the spiders and bees. This is the funny chapter – the one where we celebrate the insect's constant contribution to the fields of human comedy, recreation and day-to-day entertainment.

So let's start with some fun, fly-related facts. First up, Lady Gaga's hat. The fashionable one.

1. Flies in fashion

It was July 2011, and one of the final episodes of US dance reality show *So You Think You Can Dance*, Season 8. But it was also something of a special occasion and a fashionable moment for flies the world over. Why? Because Lady Gaga was a guest judge.

The Lady arrived in a red Versace suit complete with red leather military hat, red platform boots and green, waist-length wig. It's a difficult look to upstage. But upstage it she did by dissolving into tears after one competitor's particularly emotional performance.

Lady Gaga crying. That's an even more difficult look to upstage. But upstage it something did: a big, black fly crawling around on her red leather hat.

The world sat up and took notice. How could they not, when the fly was magnified bigger and blacker in the extreme close-up of Gaga's tears? Fashion bloggers blogged about it almost as much as the red suit and green wig. Celeb watchers sniped about it: 'And how great was that fly that settled on Lady Gaga's red cap as she was expressing what seemed like a genuine connection to the material?' wrote one. 'The insect added a perfect dash of levity and humour to the saccharine moment.'

It also added an accessory to Gaga's look. It wasn't intentional. Although, considering the singer's fashion sense, it could have been. Or still could be, one day, some day. She has worn a fire-breathing bra, a giant egg and even a dress made of raw meat. Why not a fly? Why not, indeed?

Only a single pair of flylashes was ever created. The artist allegedly pulled individual legs off dead flies, selected the best-looking ones and glued them to her own eyelids.

That's probably exactly what progressive UK artist Jessica Harrison asked herself when creating her own fly-related beauty accessories in August 2010. She called them flylashes. No prizes for guessing where they go.

More fly-catching than eye-catching, only a single pair was ever completed. In a fashion move worthy of Lady Gaga, Harrison allegedly pulled individual legs off the bodies of dead flies, selected the nicest-looking ones (whatever nice-looking flies' legs look like) and glued them to her own eyelids. Then she posted a video of the fluttering lashes online. People were shocked. Especially the People for Ethical Treatment of Animals (PETA).

'I can see how she might find tiny flies' legs to be reminiscent of human eyelashes,' said a PETA representative, 'but couldn't she just leave it at that? I mean, my beagle Lulu had ears that felt just like velvet, but that didn't inspire me to go around hacking off hounds' ears to make a beagle blazer.'

The artist pulled the video and echoed the ethical and medical concerns around fly-eye contact. 'Flies do naturally carry disease,' said Harrison, 'and I was lucky not to contract an eye infection.' Hope Gaga was listening.

Nevertheless, flies do not have to be dead or dismembered to contribute to fashion. In some circles they are simply inspiring it, indirectly, and from a safe distance. For example, at fly fishing stores all over America. No longer just for anglers and outdoorsmen, these stores are now destinations for hordes of hairstylists and general stylistas. They come in search of long, colourful fly-fishing feathers. Not to tie into fishing flies, but rather to use as hair extensions and tie to their heads.

Clearly, flies have inspired the feathery lures that are essential tools of the fly-fishing trade (more on that in point 2). But now these fishing flies are inspiring head-turning heads of hair. In 2011, reports in *The New York Times* and *The Seattle Times* touched on this new trend and its repercussions on the fly-feather farming community. In short, very specific feathers (also called 'hackles') are painstakingly grown for more than a year on the behinds of pampered roosters, who are then euthanised and plucked. It's a slow process, but the resultant plumes are perfect for fly-tying and hair-extending – they can even be brushed, blowdried, straightened and curled.

Very specific feathers, or hackles, are grown for more than a year on the behinds of pampered roosters, who are then euthanised and plucked. The resultant plumes are perfect for fly-tying and hair-extending alike.

The result? Suddenly the feather supply can't meet the demand and the price of hackles is being hiked right up. This time the flies may be safe, but the fishermen (and the roosters) are suffering at the hands of fashion.

Last in this fashion line-up, we look at sunglasses and flies. No, not fly-inspired sunglasses (those come later, in the Flies in Music section), but rather a pair of real sunglasses designed especially to shade the eyes of a fly. Seriously. There are pictures to prove it.

In 2005 a German manufacturer used ultrafast micro-lasers to build a teeny, tiny, micro set of fly-wear, which was then fitted (very carefully) onto a fly's two millimetre head.

In 2005, German manufacturer Micreon GmbH used ultrafast micro-lasers to build a teeny, tiny, micro set of fly-wear, which was then fitted (very carefully) onto a fly's two millimetre head. It made an impressive picture. Impressive enough to enter into the annual Bilder der Forschung (Photos of Science) competition. The idea was to illustrate the company's capacity to precision-make items, at scales of a fraction of a millimetre. Yes, it was something of a publicity stunt. But no matter. With custom-made shades and a much-publicised photo shoot, that was one fashionable fly posing for its close-up.

2. Flies and fishing

It's probably the most popular fly-related pursuit of them all – besides simple swatting, which we all partake in at times. It's also one of the oldest (again, besides swatting), around from at least the second century, when Macedonian fishermen reportedly tied feathers and red wool around their hooks and found much success. Since then, fake flies became to fishing what real flies are to living in Australia – an integral part of the activity. (Incidentally, it's been said that the Australian accent developed as a result of breathing through the nose to stop flies being sucked into the mouth.)

> Fly fishing can be traced back to the second century, when Macedonian fishermen reportedly tied feathers and red wool around their hooks and found much success.

The practice of using artificial flies to catch fish bobbed along nicely from 200 or so AD until the 1900s. That's when American fly fishermen in the New York Catskill Mountain streams realised they could catch even more trout if they tied their flies to look like the kind of insects that occurred naturally in the area. Turns out that fish – particularly trout – are clever and cautious enough to avoid eating a fly that doesn't look or behave like the real thing. Clearly, when it comes to fishing, fake flies make a very real difference. Particularly if they don't look fake. And thus the art of modern fly tying was born.

All artificial flies start with a hook. They always did – the hook is the backbone onto which pieces of fur, feather, hair and other natural and synthetic materials are hand-tied to create the illusion of a real fly or other insect. The flies can be classified as either imitations, which lure fish by imitating an insect as closely as possible, or attractors that are simply bright or bold enough to spur the fish to strike – like red rags arouse bulls, also destined for death. There are dry flies, tied to look like post-pupal adults at the surface, wet flies that emulate dead or drowned insects sinking below, and nymphs designed to look like the insect pupae that fish love to eat.

Nowadays thousands of artificial fly styles are being tied. Or even tens of thousands. A buffet of fake fish foods from which to pick. The poor fish knows the difference only when the very real hook is lodged in its gullet. Which is exactly the point. Unless you are coarse fishing, of course. It's called coarse fishing because, in the early 1800s, the British gentry were as snobby about freshwater fish as they were about everything else. Salmon and trout were more desirable and considered game fish. Everything else was just called coarse fish. The class structure was alive and well in rivers and streams.

Coarse-fish specific fishing techniques evolved along with the taste (or the need) for coarser fish. These include throwing bait into the water, dangling it from a float or anchoring it to a sinker (called legering). Bright lures can also be used and even fly-fishing techniques work only for certain types of fish. But the bait is the key. And one of the best coarse fish baits is a handful of maggots – real ones, not fake.

Fly larvae are the second most popular coarse fishing bait in the UK. They can be used dead or alive, impaled on a hook (carefully, or they will burst) or simply poured into the water.

This is why fly larvae are farmed in large numbers to supply the sport. In fact, they constitute the second most popular coarse fishing bait in the UK. That's according to specialist website Worms Direct, from which you can buy red, white or mixed maggots by the pint (for about £5.50) or by the gallon (for £29.95).

'Most fish prefer maggots, including bream, roach, barbel, chub, tench and carp,' says the site. 'Our maggots are fresh, clean and very lively!' Lively they may be, but they are also very mature – a polite way of saying they are already on the verge of becoming pupae or (in fishing terms) casters. Fortunately, older age works in their favour. Or, rather, in the fisherman's favour because fish love casters – particularly their crunchy shells. 'Caster maggots are not old maggots due to be thrown out!' the site explains. 'The warming up they experience in travelling is enough to start the process of pupating; on arrival keep them warm and the process will continue giving you fresh casters within a few hours.'

The larvae can be used dead or alive, impaled on a hook (carefully, or they are liable to burst) or simply poured into the water. They can also be flavoured for even more appeal. But, however they are used, the coarse fish are likely to bite.

According to *Angling Times* online, sometimes dead maggots are still better than live ones. Why? Because 'live maggots will sink to the bottom and wriggle away into the silt.' The solution, says the mag, is to kill them – pour half a pint into a polythene bag, squeeze out the air, seal it and store in the freezer for a day. 'But don't put more than half pint in each bag,' it warns. Because maggot masses generate such great amounts of heat, 'the ones in the middle will remain warm enough to stay alive.'

The tips on maggotocide continue. If you are not freezing them, you can try scalding: 'A quick way to get a handful of dead maggots for hookbaits while you are at your swim is to pour a little hot tea or coffee over a few. This will scald them and they will stiffen up and die.' So quick. So easy. Especially considering that no fishing trip is complete without a handy thermos of tea. Something for fisherman and maggot to share.

'A quick way to get a handful of dead maggots for hookbaits while you are at your swim is to pour a little hot tea or coffee over a few' — *Angling Times* online

3. Fly jokes

'Time flies like an arrow. Fruit flies like a banana,' said Groucho Marx. But he is only one of many jokesters who have taken advantage of the fly's comedy flair.

Why do flies chase garbage trucks?
They love fast food!

What do you call a fly with a sore throat?
A hoarse fly

How many flies does it take to screw in a light bulb?
Two, but how the heck do they get in there?

Come on, it's irresistible. Just about everything about the fly's looks and lifestyle is a corny pun or punchline waiting to happen. Particularly when it comes to waiters and bowls of soup.

A woman walked into the kitchen to find her husband stalking around with a flyswatter.
'What are you doing?' she asked.
'Hunting flies,' he responded.
'Killed any?' she asked.
'Yep, three males, two females,' he replied.
Intrigued she asked, 'How can you tell?'
He responded 'Three were on a beer can, two were on the phone.'

They are as classic as the road-crossing chicken jokes. And probably just about as cheesy, too. Which is why they have even been sandwiched together by some jokers...

Why did the maggot cross the road?
To get to the dead chicken.

A comedic moment that's also biologically correct.

4. Flies on film

The horror of a fly in full-colour zoom certainly hasn't been lost on Hollywood. The 1986 horror film *The Fly* won an Academy Award for Best Make-up. It also made actor Jeff Goldblum a star.

Funny from a distance. Frightening up close. The horror of a fly in full-colour zoom certainly hasn't been lost on Hollywood. Consider *The Fly*, a 1958 cult horror film in which a scientist tinkers with teleportation and ends up trading body parts with a fly that gets stuck in his machine. It was yet another laboratory-blunder story. A hybrid-hero-monster that could sit on the same shelf as *Spiderman* and *The Hulk*. But this one was more horror than hero. Something about *The Fly* made it a more monstrous monster by far.

So satisfyingly gruesome was the subject matter that *The Fly* spawned two sequels – *Return of the Fly* in 1959 and *Curse of the Fly* in 1965. Almost 20 years later, it led to a 1986 remake starring Jeff Goldblum as the freaky, fly-headed scientist turned monster. The film won an Academy Award for Best Make-up. It also made Goldblum a star.

Fast-forward to July 2009 when Barack Obama swatted a fly during an interview on live TV (remember that from Chapter 2?). American pundit and funnyman Stephen Colbert had a lot to say about it during the `Murder in the White House' segment on his show *The Colbert Report*. And so did Jeff Goldblum, who made a special appearance on this very apt episode.

'These majestic creatures have been around for 65 million years,' said Goldblum as the violins swelled. 'Isn't it possible, just possible that they have something to teach us? All they want is to be loved. And to feed on our waste. So, instead of swatting them with our hands, we should be holding them in our hearts. After all, someone who started out as a fly may go on to such great things as *Jurassic Park*, *Independence Day* and *Law & Order: Criminal Intent*. Mr President, apologise for this brutal act of violence. There can never be enough apologies.'

'All they want is to be loved. And to feed on our waste. So, instead of swatting them with our hands,
we should be holding them in our hearts.' —
Actor Jeff Goldblum on *The Colbert Report*

Wise words from The Fly himself. With proboscis lodged firmly in his cheek.

5. Flies in music

I've watched you change
Into a fly
I looked away
You were on fire
I watched a change
In you
It's like you never
Had wings
Now you feel
So alive
I've watched you change
I took you home
Set you on the glass
I pulled off your wings
Then I laughed ...

Sounds about right. A dark song with an even darker muse. Called *Change (In the House of Flies)* this turning-point song by American alternative band Deftones was released in 2000 as the first single from their album *White Pony*. It might be about pulling the wings of flies (and then laughing about it), but it's the band's most commercially successful single to date. It's also not the first time flies have inspired musicians with a taste for the macabre.

Halo of Flies was a 1973 song by iconic rockstar Alice Cooper. Granted, it was actually about spies, not flies, but the catchy name was adopted by US noise rock band Halo of Flies in the 1980s. Musically, this was something of a fly-infested time. In the same decade, UK electronic band Depeche Mode released the song Fly on the Windscreen ...

Death is everywhere
There are flies on the windscreen
For a start

Reminding us
We could be torn apart
Tonight

Poor flies. They just can't escape darkness and destruction. Even in metaphors. Even in the arts. But then, in 1991, someone finally wrote flies into a love song. Well, a sort of a love song: The Fly by U2.

A man will beg
A man will crawl
On the sheer face of love
Like a fly on a wall

It's a quick mention in a single verse – the song is actually about a phone call from someone in hell who really likes being there. But it was a significant moment for the band and the insect alike. Why? Because this first single from the album *Achtung Baby* introduced U2's new harder-edged 90s' sound to the world. Quite appropriately it arrived on the back of a fly.

Bono even commented that guitarist The Edge's playing in the song was like, 'a fly had broken into your brain and was buzzing around'. But the song also metamorphosed Bono by launching one of his new performance personas: The Fly, an archetypal strutting rock star, sheathed in leather, machismo and massive wraparound sunglasses.

For most of U2's 1992 Zoo TV Tour Bono was an alter ego called The Fly. An archetypal strutting rock star, sheathed in leather, machismo and massive wraparound sunglasses.

For most of U2's 1992 Zoo TV Tour (as well as some press conferences), Bono was not Bono, but The Fly. He was arrogant, swaggering, abrasive, dark – quite different from the intense, pious muso of the 1980s. And then there were the sunglasses. Perhaps Bono and The Fly's biggest contribution of all.

> As I write this sentence there is a fly on my computer screen. It's probably the only fly in the world that goes exactly where I tell it to with just a small shift of the wrist.

Today, Bono is still all sunglasses. Onstage or off, they seem to have become part of his anatomy. 'I'm the Imelda Marcos of sunglasses,' he told *Rolling Stone* magazine in 2005. '... It's part vanity, it's part privacy and part sensitivity.' Yes, he has 'very sensitive eyes to light', but he also just loves shades. And it's thought that his fly alter ego is where that love affair really began.

So, in some way, the fly has influenced one of the most influential artists and people of our time. No other insect could possibly boast that.

6. Fly toys

As I write this sentence there is a fly on my computer screen. Really, there is. It hovers over links as I click. It glides over words as I highlight. It's probably the only fly in the world that goes exactly where I tell it to with just a small shift of the wrist. I love it. I feel like the Pied Piper of flies. Okay fine, it's actually a fly-shaped cursor I downloaded free online. It seemed like the most natural thing to do when writing a book about flies. Plus it's actually quite sweet.

That's the thing, flies can be sweet when given half a chance. Maybe that's why The Tapir Preservation Fund is selling fly- and maggot-shaped teddy bears to raise money for endangered species and environments. Honestly. But they also sell stuffed fleas, dust mites, bed bugs, mosquitoes, scorpions and swine flu viruses, so clearly nothing is out of bounds.

'This engaging, realistic-looking stuffed housefly is soft and endearing,' says the online store. 'The legs are made of soft, plush fabric. This allows for a myriad of positions. The tips are covered with soft plastic that can't scratch small children. The body is jet-black with shimmering, rainbow-coloured wings. It has large, bulging, burgundy plush eyes. The housefly rests quietly in your hands.'

How sweet is that? Probably the first time a fly has been described as 'resting quietly' or 'soft and endearing'. And most likely the last.

The maggot-bear on the other hand is described as 'cuddly'. A cuddly maggot. That's also a first. 'Our maggot has a kindly expression and promises not to gross you out too much,' it continues. 'Have you noticed how some guys call each other 'Maggot'? What could be a more perfect gift?'

What indeed? Unless you want a photo of dead flies peeing on a wall (see point 7).

7. Fly in art

He is been called Flychelangelo (there really is a fly pun for every possible occasion). But he is really a Swedish photographer called Magnus Muhr. He photographs people, animals, nature, insects, anything really – including dead flies that he arranges in hand-drawn scenes of dancing, diving, gardening, sun tanning and peeing on walls with glee.

"I went for a walk, and found a dead fly on the ground. When I got home I put flies in comic poses on white paper, then drew the legs and background with a pencil and photographed them." -- Photographer Magnus `Flychelangelo' Muhr

It started a couple of years ago at a dull party. 'I was bored and went for a walk, then I found a dead fly on the ground,' Muhr told the *Daily Mail*. 'When I got home I put some flies in comic poses on white paper, then drew the legs and background with a pencil and photographed them.'

Easy as that, Flychelangelo was born. Now Muhr is constantly collecting fly carcasses from light fittings and windows (he never kills them), and his growing collection of dead-fly art is getting laughs all over the world. There are dead-fly Cossack dancers, horse riders, track athletes and Sumo wrestlers. There are groups of them getting drunk and queues of them lining up outside public bathrooms. There are even dead flies looking at photos of dead flies. Each one is funnier than the next.

'I think they have become popular as they are very simple and don't need any text,' Muhr says. 'The language is international and the humour alludes to human feelings and activities.'

Flies are funny because they make us feel more human and more alive. Even when the are dead. Bet Jim Carrey can't do that.

8. Fly-powered planes

The FlyPower® kit contains everything you need. Well, almost. For $5.95 you get full instructions and the pieces and parts for two aircraft. Super Glue® is not included. And neither is the `engine' (read: fly). This you have to catch yourself. Then you have to glue the fly to your handmade plane and prepare for take-off. It's easier said than done, but the folks at online fly-powered plane store, FlyPower®, are full of helpful tips.

> Flies are very sensitive to temperature, and apparently a quick freeze is very useful for people who are 'unfamiliar with handling flies and other smaller life forms'. Which is just about everyone these days.

Like this one: 'Several readers and even a few scholars have proposed the judicious use of cryogenics to make the flies easier to handle,' they suggest. 'Basically this involves putting your engine in the freezer for a very short period of time (20 to 60 seconds) [to] facilitate the handling in the process of mounting and gluing.'

We know that flies are very sensitive to temperature. And apparently this quick freeze is very useful for people who are 'unfamiliar with handling flies and other smaller life forms'. Which is just about everyone these days – although it hasn't always been the case.

FlyPower® judiciously tracks the history of insect-powered flight, from inventor Nikola Tesla's June bug-powered motor in the late 1800s to the first prototype fly-powered plane built in 1949 by a scientist who used wood for the fuselage and Lucky Strike cigarette cellophane for wings. This is the model that FlyPower® still uses today. But they have turned the science into a high-flying art.

'Talk to your engine (read: fly) during the mounting process,' says another handy hint. 'It seems to calm them down somewhat, and sets the mood for the rest of their day. They also seem to be partial to classical music and/or The Doors. We don't understand why but it's true. Resuscitation of your engine is critical. Do not place under a heat lamp or other heat source. Once mounted to the engine, you can breathe gently onto the engine to awaken him/her. You will find you can achieve better results if this is done prior to brushing your teeth in the morning. They love it!'

Who would have thought it? Flies love morning breath and The Doors' music. But, if you want them to tow a little plane and make you feel like an avionic engineer, it helps to give them exactly what they want. That's what FlyPower® is all about. They believe in good `engine maintenance' (or fly care) and promote a policy of compassion and `catch and release'.

'Be careful in your handling of the fly,' the site advises finally. 'They are precision instruments and as such are delicate. When you have finished using your plane, take a small pair of scissors and snip off the engine mount as close to the body as possible. It won't make a damn bit of difference to the fly, but you may feel better.'

The first prototype fly-powered plane was built in 1949 by a scientist who used wood for the fuselage and Lucky Strike cigarette cellophane for wings.

On the one hand the carnivorous clock is a power-saving invention that runs on alternative fuel and helps to control pests. On the other, it's a fly-slaying gizmo that feeds a morbid fascination.

You certainly will. How else do you say: 'Thank you for flying with us' to a fly?

9. Fly-powered clock

For forensic anthropologists, flies on a dead body constitute a bioclock that tells the time since death. For UK designers James Auger and Jimmy Loizeau, flies on a piece of flypaper constitute biofuel for an actual clock that uses their dead bodies to tell the time until dinner. Hard to say which one is weirder. Probably Auger and Loizeau's. It's a robotic carnivorous clock. Eight dead flies can power it for 12 whole days.

The design is doubly clever. The first clever part is a honey-coated rotating belt that attracts and traps flies like a regular piece of flypaper. The stuck flies are then rotated, very slowly, towards a blade that scrapes them into the second clever part, a Microbial Fuel Cell (MFC), which transforms the organic fly matter into electrical energy that powers the digital clock.

'A fly buzzing around the window suddenly becomes an actor in a live game of life,' Auger has been quoted as saying. 'The viewer half wills it towards the robot and half hopes for it to escape.' So, on the one hand this is a power-saving invention that runs on an alternative fuel source and helps control pests. On the other, it's a fly-slaying gizmo that feeds a morbid fascination as much as it does an MFC.

It's like a carnivorous plant – we're fascinated and sickened by it simultaneously. In fact, that's what influenced the designers. Carnivorous plants, like the ever-entertaining Venus flytrap. That's also why they call their clock an entertainment robot. And they have made others too, like a robotic fly and moth-attracting lampshade that provides light, and a mouse-trap coffee table that lures mice into a table leg with food and then consumes them in a fuel cell that powers an LED screen.

When it comes to morbid fascination, a mouse-eating table definitely trumps a fly-trapping clock. But both are still prototypes. That said, it's just a matter of time before the design is refined to be more fly-efficient. And time flies when you're using dead flies to tell the time.

CHAPTER 10

SAVING THE WORLD

ONCE UPON A TIME in 2009 someone spotted a housefly at Mount Everest base camp. Big deal, you might say. That's not a fairy tale. It's an everyday occurrence, just set at an exotic location. But it is a big deal – in fact a much bigger deal than being at the foot of the highest mountain in the world. Particularly for Nepali mountain climber Dawa Steven Sherpa, who runs regular expeditions in the Himalayas and works as a World Wildlife Fund (WWF) ambassador on climate change. He is the one who saw the fly. And that's how this fairy tale begins.

It might start with 'once upon a time', but that doesn't mean it ends with 'happily ever after'.

'It's happened twice this year,' Steven told *The Guardian* newspaper at the time, referring to the fly spotting. But the presence of even one or two houseflies at an altitude of over 5,000 metres is so much more than simply a nuisance for climbers and guides. 'What I do is climb. It's a family business,' Steven explained. 'And what we see is the Himalayan glaciers melting ... [at] an average of 10 to 20 metres a year. It's not a seasonal thing anymore. It's rapid. It's so apparent.'

Even the summit of Everest is shrinking. 'You used to be able to get 50 people on the ridge to it,' he said. 'Now there is room for 18 people at most. The cornice is breaking off. A big crevasse is opening. It seems nothing is safe anymore.'

Nothing indeed. Climate change is an insidious, insect-like thing that's crawling and flying its way into every nook and cranny of modern life. In addition to melting glaciers and shrinking summits, it's also causing more insects to crawl and fly their way into more areas of our Earth. Like flies to Everest base camp — and some places closer to home.

According to a 2005 report in the British Ecological Society's Journal of Applied Ecology, if current climate change predictions are correct, the UK could be heading for a housefly population explosion. Some might call it a plague. Either way it doesn't sound good. For four years, researchers from the University of Southampton caught over 100,000 flies in about 10,000 sticky traps and concluded that if temperatures increase the predicted 5°C by 2080, fly populations in the UK will probably expand by a mammoth 250 percent. This does not bode well for future picnics in the park. But, although fly infestation might be a symptom of our environmental ills, it could also be a solution in disguise.

If temperatures increase the predicted 5° C by 2080, fly populations in the UK will probably expand by a mammoth 250%. This does not bode well for future picnics in the park.

Consider once again the over-fishing of our seas. It's an environmental crisis leading to a potential dietary deficit of note. In order to generate enough farm animal protein (like fish, chicken and pork) to feed humans, we need enough animal protein (like fishmeal) to feed the animal cities we have built. Think back to the big, scary numbers on the opening pages of this book. Numbers like 30 percent – the percentage of all fish caught that ends up as fishmeal for farmed monogastric animals like poultry, pigs and other fish. Or 2.3 kg – the amount of marine-caught fish needed to produce only 1 kg of farmed fish, 70 percent of which ends up as waste. It seems the scariest numbers are swimming around fish farming or aquaculture itself. It's an inherently unsustainable industry. Which is why it has to change.

More scary numbers: the 2007 Worldwatch Institute report Oceans in Peril says that shrimp farming uses around 2.5 times more fishmeal than the amount of shrimp ultimately produced. That's nothing compared to tuna – when wild tuna are rounded up and fattened in sea pens, the fish-feed input is a massive 20 times greater than the weight output that results. Unsustainable is an understatement. In order to be considered sustainable, an aquaculture operation would need to fulfil various criteria, including not using fishmeal or fish oil-based feeds from unsustainable fisheries and not being responsible for a net fish-protein loss.

When Greenpeace says that there aren't really any sustainable species of fish in aquaculture, it's a clear message that something is broken in the system itself. Which it is — although hopefully not beyond repair.

When Greenpeace says that there aren't really any sustainable species of fish in aquaculture, it's a clear message that something is broken in the system itself.

It's simple: fishmeal never was and no longer is the ideal meal for fish and other monogastric farm animals. Similarly, because its production relies on huge amounts of land, water and fuel, non-marine protein like soya doesn't make a very sustainable alternative (plus it contains fewer essential amino acids than marine protein, meaning these have to be made, brought in and added). Add to this the fact that there are more people on the planet than ever, hungering for ever more food at the lowest possible price. Clearly, we need a protein source that's dirt-cheap, common as muck and sustainable enough to help save the planet. Where on Earth will we find something like that?

If you are reading this book (or at least this page), the answer is right in front of you. It's the fly. The title gives it away. *The Story of the Fly and How It Could Save the World*. In short, the fly could save the world by supplying a sustainable source of protein from existing waste nutrients, which will help save the fish in the seas. Well, the fly and the maggot (or larva, as it is more properly known) – the protein comes from the larvae, and the larvae come from the flies.

All things going as they should, this new (or rather time-honoured and natural) protein could eliminate the need for fishmeal trawling altogether. And that's the happiest possible ending for this story of human and fly. Because humans are the third character in this story. More specifically, a group of humans who have started a company called AgriProtein in South Africa.

WHY THE HUMANS ARE DOING IT

If this story is a fairy tale, there would have to be at least one magic character – like a magician, or an alchemist. Someone who wears a pointy hat and turns one thing into another: spun thread into gold, or an ugly frog into a handsome prince. The humans at AgriProtein don't wear pointy hats. But they do turn one thing into another – more specifically, something quite worthless into something of great social and environmental value. It is a kind of alchemy – in a complex of sealed cages and large sheds just outside Cape Town, dead animal blood becomes live animal food. That doesn't sound very pleasant. Better to call it bioconversion or nutrient recycling, through which organic waste from abattoirs is transformed into an edible, natural protein for farmed fish, shrimps, poultry and pigs. The transforming force is the life cycle of the fly. That sounds so much more pleasant. But the environmental benefit is exactly the same.

These days, we reuse and recycle everything. We happily breathe new life into waste paper, plastic, metals and glass. It isn't such a strange idea. Why not recycle nutrients too?

These days, recycling is an almost automatic step in the using and discarding process. We consciously reuse more and misuse less. We happily breathe new life into waste paper, plastic, metals and glass. It isn't such a strange idea. Why not reincarnate nutrients too? Think about it: it takes the same amount of resources (like diesel, land and water) to make all the bits of a chicken that end up on a plate as it takes to make those that don't. Then we go and throw the bits we don't like away. It's such a waste – unless you can put those free discarded bits to good use. Like recycling meat-industry waste into meat-industry fuel. That's where the AgriProtein approach comes in.

The company farms flies and feeds the growing larvae with abattoir waste. The fattened-up larvae are then dried and milled into a protein-rich, powdery product – a maggot meal that's on par with fishmeal, and nutritionally better than soya. Appropriately, it's called Magmeal.

It contains 17 amino acids – nine of which are essential ones – with similar lysine, methonine, threonine and tryptophane levels (and higher cystine levels) than marine fishmeal. It's more complete than soya, which delivers only eight amino acids in its plant protein package. That's why Magmeal makes an ideal animal feed, especially for animals that eat larvae naturally and by choice.

That said, it's not as straightforward as it sounds. Yes, fly larvae love blood and dead body parts. And yes, birds and fish love the larvae that love the blood. That's the natural part. But it isn't natural to ask flies and larvae to live and love together in massive numbers and on an industrial scale. AgriProtein is taking the natural process and industrialising it – as has already been done with other farm animals, such as cows, chickens and pigs. The aim is to optimise the larval living and feeding conditions and to develop a plant that can pump out enough Magmeal to start supplying the farming industry's huge requirements. Each factory will produce 100 tonnes of wet larvae or 20 tonnes of dried, protein-rich larvae per day. And that's just one plant.

The aim is to pump out enough Magmeal to start supplying the farming industry's huge requirements. Each plant will produce 100 tonnes of wet larvae or 20 tonnes of dried, protein-rich larvae per day.

There is a great deal of international interest in this innovative feed. Probably because, as yet, no one else is making it. Other than Mother Nature. But even she needs help cranking up the crop.

The idea of farming flies and larvae is not nearly as new as the idea of doing so for agricultural, environmental and commercial gain. People have been growing larvae for recreational coarse fishing and some even to feed exotic pet birds and their koi carp. But talk is cheap and action more expensive. Besides a few smaller-scale and some academic projects, no one has really put much time or money into the industrial fly and larval farming process.

It simply hasn't been urgent enough. But things have changed and urgent is now where we're at.

While ruminants or multigastric animals like cattle, sheep and goats can make good on protein from grain or grass (and while their feed has been produced industrially for a long while), monogasts such as fish, shrimp, chicken and pigs need more complex animal or animal-like protein to meet their nutritional needs. Chicken can be successfully fed with plant-based protein supplemented with specific amino acids or fishmeal. On the other hand, fish like salmon and trout and crustaceans like shrimps and prawns need the dense protein of fishmeal to grow.

When the oil price was stable and the oceans were overflowing with fish, there wasn't any need to develop industrial monogastric protein plans. But now oil is more pricy and fish stocks more dicey by the day. Sustainable protein is a serious priority. Bring on the maggot meal.

WHY THE FLY IS THE HERO

Flies breed like rabbits. In fact, it might be more accurate to say that rabbits (as well as anything that reproduces excessively) actually breed like flies. That's what makes flies the heroes of this new nutrient-recycling process. They breed like flies. And they mature fast too.

A quick recap: a female housefly lays an egg, which hatches into a larva. This quite featureless larva grows quickly and reaches pupation, ready for metamorphosis to adult flyhood, in just 72 hours. In fact, if conditions are correct, it will gain over 400 times its weight in these few days. This lightning-speed life cycle is another of the fly's heroic features. From start to finish, it's over in less than 21 days. So scientists can try things faster, see the effects sooner and absorb the inevitable mistakes more quickly, cheaply and far less painfully than with a longer-living guinea pig, which can survive up to eight years. This means that, if you were farming guinea pigs, it would take 96 times longer to assess production methods than it does when you are farming flies. Even if guinea pigs made great guinea pigs and a good protein source, who has that kind of time when trying to save the world?

Some flies are better at recycling certain nutrients. The blow fly, black soldier fly and housefly will all quite gladly transform our waste into their own larval body-part protein. Although each fly does has its favourite waste on which to feed.

In any case, not all flies are made for the same sort of world-saving heroics. Some flies are better at recycling certain nutrients. The blowfly, the black soldier fly and the common housefly will all quite gladly eat most forms of waste and turn it into their own larval body-part protein. But each has a favoured waste on which to feed. Some prefer rotting flesh while others prefer rotting veg. There is no accounting for taste.

Blowflies have already been used for nutrient recycling. As have black soldier flies. They are veritable mercenaries of waste management. Black soldier fly larvae made a successful protein source for catfish and tilapia (in 1987) and (in 1977) a protein supplement for pigs. In 2006 they got a registered trademark in the US and a more glamorous brand name – Phoenix Worms – under which they are sold as live feed for zoo animals and exotic pets. They are also marketed as catchy-sounding Soldier Grubs (great for pet feeding and composting), Reptiworms (developed specifically for the producers' bearded dragon collection) and Calciworms (due to a high calcium content believed to build the bones of the animals that eat them).

Clearly, armies of black soldier larvae are already hard at work as small-scale nutrient recyclers. But they are also much larger-scale waste managers – especially on farms where manure piles up more quickly than the flies that swarm in to find it. Black soldier fly larvae have an most unquenchable appetite for organic waste, such as manure and rotting vegetables. They churn it up and dissolve it into smaller, more liquid piles – before it has time to start rotting and making even more of a mess.

In 2011 in Spain, 20 million black soldier larvae process a tonne of zoo-animal waste per day.

In 2011 in Spain, 20 million black soldier larvae process a tonne of zoo-animal waste per day. A tonne a day! That's faster and more efficient than even the most energetic earthworms or any other band of compost creators. These Spanish soldiers were part of a pilot project by the University of Alicante. Results showed that they could eliminate about 90 percent of the animal excreta and waste, leaving just 10 percent for conversion into organic fertiliser. Researchers also see potential to use this 10 percent residue in biodiesel, pharmaceuticals or even aquaculture feed.

Pretty encouraging, then, that black soldier larvae are thought to have the capacity to cut farm-animal waste in the US by an estimated 25 percent. Farmers love them for that. They have fallen for the maggots' ability to shrink mounds of manure, manage odour and stave off common pests. Because the soldiers render manure more liquid, they make it a less appealing place for other flies to lay their eggs. It's a neat feature that's not lost on the Spanish researchers, either.

'Our research group has developed protocols for breeding and selection of different species,' says coordinator Professor Santos Rojo. He explains that this could allow the technology to be applied to 'a variety of waste and organic by-products from various sources – food and agriculture industry, meat-processing and catering waste'.

Who knows, one day human waste may yet be managed by larvae and flies. To this end, AgriProtein (and some of their unusual flies) are adding their expertise to Sanitation Ventures – a consortium supported by the Bill and Melinda Gates Foundation that's working towards hygienic innovations for pit latrines and other on-site sanitation systems in developing countries around the world. Through this and other projects, flies are fast becoming more loved and appreciated for their way with human and other waste. The housefly, especially, deserves a bit more love.

Housefly larvae already have one agricultural activity on their to-do lists. It's broadly related to their medical to-do's. The maggot debridement and inhalation therapies discussed in Chapter 5 are indicative of the larvae's in-built antibacterial effect. This effect is even active against antibiotic-resistant bacteria like strains of Methicillin-resistant *Staphylococcus aureus* (MRSA) and Vancomycin-resistant *Enterococci* (VRE), says a study from South Korea's Kangwon National University published in the Journal of Environmental Biology in 2010.

More than 50% of all antibiotics produced worldwide end up being given preventatively to chickens on industrial farms.

For a farmer, any bacterium is a farm-wide bloodbath waiting to happen. But an antibiotic-resistant bacterium is more horrific by far, simply because it's more difficult to treat. The antibiotics themselves are to blame. Or rather the antibiotic overuse – more than 50 percent of all antibiotics produced worldwide are given preventatively to chickens on farms. The result? Bacteria are evolving and becoming progressively resistant to our antibiotic panacea. Which is why many smaller farmers are moving towards organic farming and drug- and chemical-free methods that may address the problem at its root.

'Extracts from fly maggots can potently inhibit MRSA and VRE strains,' the Kangwon National University study concludes – a conclusion that could be helpful for the development of natural antibacterial agents for organic farming. But that's not all. According to a patent application for the housefly larvae extract, there are other benefits to this antibiotic additive for feed:

'[It's] prepared using housefly larvae, which contain 50 percent or higher crude protein and are thus a good protein source, capable of replacing soybean meal and fishmeal for broiler and layer chickens,' says the patent application. 'Thus, the feed additive promotes the growth of beneficial bacteria and inhibits the growth of harmful bacteria in the gut, thereby having probiotic effects identical to or greater than those of conventional fructooligosaccharides.'

In other words, just as they help kill bad bacteria, the housefly larvae provide growth-promotion for good bacteria and lots of protein. Protein, glorious protein. This brings us back to the next agricultural aim on the housefly's superhero list.

'For the use of larvae as a potential high-quality protein source, the housefly from the order *Diptera* is probably the most suitable organism to use,' says South African animal nutritionist Dr Elsje Pieterse. Firstly, this is because houseflies are more abundantly available than just about anything else. Secondly, it's because housefly protein is created more explosively fast than just about anything else.

Dr Pieterse is with the Department of Animal Sciences at the University of Stellenbosch. She is also a member of the AgriProtein advisory board. She explains that, 'the black soldier fly larvae contain significantly less protein than the housefly larvae. Also, the complete larval life cycle of the housefly at a typical temperature of 30°C is under three days, compared to 14 days for the black soldier fly.'

In the black soldier versus housefly speed race, the latter is clearly winning.

The aim is to match the waste to the fly. Blood is best disposed of by houseflies, while starches and stomach contents are better fed to black soldiers.

The housefly matures faster and yields more of the edible end-product that makes the whole venture worthwhile. But the aim is to match the waste to the fly – blood is best disposed of by houseflies, while starches and stomach contents are better fed to black soldiers. The research has spoken. AgriProtein is listening. When it comes to recycling abattoir blood waste, the housefly is the bug of choice.

WHAT THEY PUT IN

Boring thread. Ugly frog. Plain pumpkin. You simply can't get spun gold, a handsome prince or a carriage to get to the ball without them. Every fairy-tale act of alchemy demands that the alchemist makes something magical out of something quite mundane. And it's this mundane something that makes all the difference. We think it's the carriage that carries Cinderella to her ever-after. But it's actually the pumpkin. The plain old pumpkin is the key.

The same applies when you are farming flies and making larval protein. You need something mundane to put into the pot and start the magic process. Or rather into the bucket of fly larvae to make them grow.

Blood, intestines, gut contents, rejected carcasses, dead-on-arrivals, carcass trimmings, heads, hooves, feet, hides, chicken feathers and chicken fat. Sounds like the makings of a maggot smorgasbord. But not all of these nutrient-rich abattoir waste products make it onto the AgriProtein menu. Some of them – like the intestines, heads and hooves – are destined for other markets and even human consumption. Therefore it's mostly the blood, fat, intestinal contents and carcasses that end up feeding the fly larvae and entering the alchemical protein pot.

Nutrient-rich abattoir waste products like blood, intestinal contents and carcasses end up feeding the fly larvae and entering the alchemical protein pot.

These are the bits that make all the difference: the plain old blood and animal parts are the key. In fact, animal blood is the lifeblood of insect rearing en masse. It's also been used as a food source for farming tsetse fly and screwworm, mostly because it's a freely available by-product of the industrial meat industry, but also because its nutrient and moisture content is just so good. Consequently, animal blood makes an excellent larval meal when combined with other nutritious things. It's called blood meal. A smoothie of nutrients. A larvae-friendly blend.

Instead of draining, burying or composting it, how much safer would it be to collect the blood and intestinal contents, crush the carcasses and mix it all into species-relevant meal that's disposed of and recycled in the larval digestive tract?

This is just another way that fly farming helps to protect the environment. In addition to sparing the fish in the sea, it mops up some of the organic waste produced by slaughterhouses. This waste is a potential health risk. If it's allowed to seep into the soil or left to ferment in trenches – as condemned carcasses sometimes are – it can spread disease and become a feeding ground for harmful bacteria. Where blood is left in pits, the haemoglobin can settle out and down, threatening to poison local water tables. Instead of draining, burying or composting it, how much safer would it be to collect the blood and intestinal contents, crush the carcasses and mix it all into a species-relevant meal that's disposed of and recycled in the larval digestive tract? It would be much, much safer. As long as the larval digestive tract is the only one it ends up in.

Abattoir blood is not meant to be eaten by animals. In many countries it's banned or restricted as an animal feed. Why? Because the blood is a possible carrier of diseases like tuberculosis, Rift Valley fever (RVF), Q fever, and anthrax. Feeding animals to one another is considered a cause of the Bovine Spongiform Encephalopathy (BSE) crisis in Europe. Nevertheless, abattoir blood can be safely fed to larvae that will ultimately be fed to the animals. The operative word is `safely' – it has to be safe for all the flies, animals and humans concerned.

First, fly safety. Of course, eating animal blood is safe for flies. These insects and their offspring are naturally adapted to seek out this precise food source and devour it with ingrained gusto. They have been dining on it since dinosaurs roamed the Earth. But the diners can be damaged if veterinary drugs or pesticides are used and remain in the blood. These substances are toxic for flies. Blood should therefore rather be irradiated to kill pathogens, although tiny infective particles called prions sometimes slip through this nuking process. This is problematic because prions are problematic – the microscopic, misshapen proteins can cause a range of diseases or Transmissible Spongiform Encephalopathies (TSEs) that affect both humans and animals. Which brings us to the second safety concern in turning abattoir blood into animal feed: animal safety.

Preventing the spread of blood-borne animal disease is not that difficult -- even if you are feeding animal blood to larvae and the self-same larvae to other animals. But you have to focus on containment. Blood sourcing is contained within a local area – and limited to areas with regular testing and little or no risk of animal disease. Similarly, blood transport and storage is limited, avoided or at least contained safely and correctly – generally blood is dried or frozen and sealed until use.

Finally, human safety. But not the humans you might think. If the animals that eat the blood-eating larvae are safe, then so are the humans who eat the meat that the larvae-eating animals become. These humans are never exposed to the blood itself. And blood-borne infections cannot pass via the maggot into the animal eating them and therefore into the food system.

Where human safety is concerned, the only people worth worrying about are the workers on the farms that produce the maggots (that feed on the meat, that's consumed by the humans, that farm the flies, that lead to the maggots, and so on).

Because they are the only humans in the chain who have direct contact with the animal blood, farm workers' protection is secured by making even more certain that blood products are locally sourced, properly stored, carefully transported and obsessively tested and decontaminated. The factories adhere to human grade food production standards like GMP (Good Management Practices), HACCP (Hazard Analysis Critical Control Point) procedures and the ISO 2200 quality standards. Which means we can proceed safely.

HOW THE MAGIC IS MADE

One thing is certain: safe and sustainable protein can't be made by waving a wand or saying a magic word. Another thing is certain: it can't be made quickly, easily or according to a recipe by magician or celebrity chef. It's a slow, seemingly unmagical process of trial and error, many trials and many, many more errors. But that doesn't make the making of it any less spellbinding. That's what the AgriProtein team discovered as they found their way.

Millions and millions of flies fill huge cages like clouds of dark, buzzing smoke. Their issue end up in the Larva Shed, where layers of larvae squirm and churn up the red-black dust of blood mixed with bran.

What's especially spellbinding is the sheer scope of the project as it unfolds at the AgriProtein development site in the Cape winelands. It's an industrial plant on a farm. A scientific hub surrounded by red earth and electric-green fields. Cows walk the dirt roads in black-and-white crowds. Vineyards fan out across the surrounding valley floor. And in this space where science and agriculture intersect, flies in a series of warehouses cycle through their metamorphic forms and states.

In the Fly House, millions and millions of flies fill huge cages like clouds of dark, buzzing smoke. Their issue end up in the Larva Shed, where layers and layers of larvae squirm and churn up the red-black dust of blood mixed with bran. Troughs and troughs of feeding larvae in rows upon rows. It's a sight to behold -- so many creatures surviving together in a synthesised system. That's the most spellbinding thing of all. Even more so for the people who have spent years working out how to make it all happen.

People like AgriProtein Researcher Manager Elaine Gloy. Part mother, part shepherd and part hotel concierge, she is the overseer of the colony's comfort and well-being. She constantly tests and assesses the fly and larval environments. She monitors behaviour and watches how growth rates spike and dip. She knows the flock – knows when they are hungry and when they are well-fed. And she uses this knowledge to constantly optimise living and feeding conditions at each age and stage. The result? 'More surviving maggots, and more Magmeal,' says Gloy. It's all in a day's work. A good day's work if everything goes well.

'One fly can lay up to 800 eggs in her life,' says AgriProtein CEO David Drew. 'Seventy-two hours later the eggs are in the larval stage and then about three days later they have turned into pupae. Four to five days after this you'll have another generation of flies and five to six days after that there are more eggs. Everything has to be optimised – temperature, moisture and the correct food for larvae and for flies. It's challenging, but, under the right conditions, it's quick and the growth is exponential.'

The aim is to yield not just the greatest possible number of larvae, but also the plumpest, healthiest, most protein-rich specimens. The kind that get farm animals gulping down gulletsful and growing at top speed.

Quick and exponential is good. But it's not good enough. The aim is to yield not just the greatest possible number of larvae, but also the plumpest, healthiest, most protein-rich specimens. The kind that get trout splashing through streams, chickens darting across roads and farm animals gulping down gulletsful and growing at top speed.

In pursuing this aim, AgriProtein is a commercial, environmental and wholly scientific enterprise. Larval testing is done through Stellenbosch University's Department of Animal Sciences. The company's advisory board includes local and international academics from an array of fields – a microbiologist from Denmark, a bioengineer from Korea and two animal nutritionists from South Africa and Singapore.

Clearly, making Magmeal is not about magic. It's about science. Which is why there are so many scientists and supervisors working on it. They are working for happier flies, happier larvae and eggs that are happier to be laid and then hatched. It's easier said than done – but it's getting done. And here's how.

THE FLIES

The first batch of AgriProtein flies was bought in October 2009 from the South African Bureau of Standards (SABS). Yes, there really is such a thing as an SABS-approved fly. The Bureau keeps a population on-hand for testing pesticides and bug sprays. A few hundred thousand more were acquired from Benin – from a breeding facility that breeds larvae and infects them with parasitic wasp eggs (the larvae are sold and the wasps hatch in the control area and go on to kill off other fly larvae).

A million or so flies produce large amounts of CO_2, which collects near the floor where the insects like to rest. Basically, they were asphyxiating themselves.

The flies started breeding, as flies are wont to do. Soon there were 200,000 per cage in a room lined with cages. But what looked like procreative success turned quickly to calamity, and a carpet of carcasses rolled out every morning. It was a mass-murder mystery that took a little while to solve. A million or so flies produce large amounts of CO_2, which collects near the floor where the insects like to rest. Basically, they were asphyxiating themselves. The solution? Better ventilation and a couple of big, powerful fans. Case closed. Well, the first case of many.

It turned out that flies were more difficult to keep and breed than was previously thought. The trials and errors piled up. So did the dead bodies as each misstep was made. It became clear that flies in captivity need three things to survive and multiply. They need food (the right kind), water (the right way) and somewhere to lay their eggs (at the right time and place). It sounds simple, but it's not. It's a lot of rights that can potentially go wrong.

'*Musca domestica* is broadly omnivorous and the material the fly is feeding on must be made into a liquid state,' says animal nutritionist Dr Elsje Pieterse. 'In adult flies sugars and starches are needed for normal longevity. Then proteins – like those from blood serum – and carbohydrates are necessary for growth in larvae and for reproduction in adults.' So, while AgriProtein larvae for harvesting are fed mostly on blood meal, their parents are spared the blood and get a special dry diet of milk powder, molasses and sugar – which they liquidise themselves with some saliva and stomach juices.

This is how the breeding population is kept sterile. No adult flies are exposed to blood or body parts. The same applies to the larvae that precede them – the ones destined for maturity and the breeding team. These larvae get sugar and milk powder while their protein-producing siblings get blood. Evidently, eating is a big part of fly and larval life. But so is drinking. It's a matter of life and death.

Flies are suicidally attracted to fluid. If there is a cup of coffee or bowl of soup on the table, they will find it and probably end up floating in it.

If you want to kill a fly, don't give it water for about 12 hours. Death by dehydration. Like all living organisms, flies need moisture to survive. But flies are also suicidally attracted to it. If there is a cup of coffee or bowl of soup on the table, they will find it and probably end up floating in it. Flies can't store much moisture in their bodies, so they constantly seek it out; they need a constant supply. That said, you can't just water them as you would horses or roses. You can't hook up a hose or bring in a bucket with a well-intentioned 'Bottoms Up'. Perhaps 'Belly Up' would be more appropriate. That's what happened at AgriProtein when buckets of water were placed in the cages – the flies dived in for a drink, or tried to take a safe sip from the edges, and still ended up drowning.

It's almost impossible to give flies water without leaving them waterlogged — or worse, drowning them.

The next idea was to leave a wet cloth on the floor – from which water could be sucked up if you have a proboscis. The flies did just that and still drowned. Their bodies are not only naturally dehydrated, but also extremely hygroscopic, or inclined to absorb moisture from anything – even from the air or a wet cloth left innocently on the floor. Poor flies. Fluid is spontaneously drawn into them through every surface. It's like their bodies are plastered with proboscises. It's almost impossible to give them water without leaving them waterlogged -- or worse, drowning them.

It's a tough one. How do you provide lots of water with lots of dry surfaces to support hygroscopic feet? After almost a year of failed attempts, the answer arrived in the post. Actually it arrived with a microscope – fortunately a very delicate piece of equipment that needs to be transported with lots of padding and care. The microscope was packed in a box full of polystyrene chips. Perfect. They were light enough to stay buoyant but solid enough to support the weight of a fly. When the chips were floated in buckets they made an archipelago of polystyrene islands, with oceans of water in between from which to drink.

Water and food were right on track. Now all that was left was the eggs.

THE EGGS

Collecting a billion microscopic eggs from a million flies laying all over a huge cage would be a daunting task for even the most nit-picky of people. The first trick is to get them all to lay in one easily accessed space. How? By creating a kind of fly-laying haven. A place or a process that ensures that all the eggs are deposited in the same area at the same time. It's possible, but calls for a whole lot of plotting and planning.

Fortunately, some of this work was done in UK and European universities between the World Wars when scientists were looking into larvae as a feed source. They identified the right attractants and moisture levels that made an egg-laying area ideal. Too wet or too dry won't do. It has to be just right. The flies also like nooks and crannies to lay in. The AgriProtein solution: a laying tray full of honeycomb-shaped cavities with six corners each, just begging to be laid in, and an attractant – like molasses – added to sweeten the deal. As long as the moisture levels are correct, this tray carries the perfect set of conditions for laying. All your eggs in one basket, whenever you want them. Just as required for fly rearing.

Somehow the eggs know what awaits them on the outside – a hearty meal or nothing more than hunger and a fight to escape it. Clever eggs. If it's the latter, they just won't come out.

The hatching is the easy part. Relative to the laying, that is. Getting the eggs to hatch into larvae needs nothing more than some kind of food nearby (which explains why flies so often lay in or around a nest of rotting waste or flesh). Somehow the eggs know what awaits them on the outside. They know if there is a hearty meal or nothing more than hunger and a fight to escape it. And if it's the latter, they just won't come out. Clever eggs.

They almost secure their own survival. They also respond to more comfortable temperatures – research has shown that a nice burst of 37°C heat and a bit of infrared light will help coax them out in the fastest possible hatching time (about seven hours).

This makes it easy for AgriProtein. Relatively. A small clump of eggs is placed on a cellulose sponge positioned in the middle of a bucket of blood meal. It's called a hatch patch. That's where they stay, incubating under infrared lights at an optimally toasty temperature, until the larvae crawl out in search of their meal. In theory, that's exactly how it happened from the word go. But in practice, well, it's not.

Hatching might be a simple act of hide and seek – hide in the egg and then come out to seek food. But egg laying, it turns out, is a very specialist ball game. The kind of ball game where everything can go wrong and does. It was all very confusing in the beginning, an ongoing larval disappearing act. Yes, the eggs were hatching in droves, but the larvae were disappearing faster than they could wriggle away from whatever was picking them off. It took a while to work it all out. The truth was unpleasant but undeniable: they were actually picking each other off. The maggots were eating one another.

For larvae, anything goes in the scramble to get ahead. Fratricide is perfectly in order. Followed by cannibalism. As long as you stick to the siblings that are smaller than you.

When you are part of a big family, you have to fight for your food, space and place in the world. Maggots apparently take this very seriously. They are highly competitive, meaning anything goes in the scramble to get ahead. Fratricide is perfectly in order. Followed by cannibalism. As long as you stick to the siblings that are smaller than you. And that's what was threatening the fabric of the AgriProtein family: the older larvae were eating the younger. Even a small age difference was enough – those born in the morning would gladly eat hatchlings from the afternoon for lunch.

But because time of hatching is determined by time of laying, that's where this problem had to be solved. At the egg-laying phase. The ball game that could topple the project as a whole.

What was needed was an egg-laying switch. Something that could flip the process on and off, like a light. In this case, it proved to be not electrical, but environmental – the laying tray, bearing the perfect conditions for egg deposition. But the timing counted too, as the AgriProtein researchers realised when they stayed up all day and night watching a cage full of flies with no tray or material in which to lay. The female flies held out as long as they could. After 33 hours, they were so desperate to oviposit that they just did – anywhere and everywhere. From this the team deduced that if you provide an egg-laying window of opportunity, flies will go straight through it. They will even store up their eggs (as long as they can) and wait for the tray of prime conditions to come.

The new plan: slide the tray into the cage once a day, three times a week for 10 minutes at a time. It's like a nudge and a wink. The flies take the hint and the eggs are laid at the same time and place. The larvae, when they hatch, are then all the same age and don't eat each other. Egg laying and larval cannibalism solved. Like two flies with one swat.

Sadly for many, there is no such thing as a switch for getting laid. But this system is probably almost as good.

THE LARVAE

If maggots dream about going to heaven, it probably looks like a restaurant garbage can glistening in the sun, or else the AgriProtein Larva Shed. Both are the perfect physical embodiment of every possible larval need. The only difference is that the garbage can is a product of

If maggots dream about going to heaven, it probably looks like a restaurant garbage can glistening in the sun, or else the AgriProtein Larva Shed.

chance (and lots of leftovers), while the Larva Shed is a conscious, human-made, maggot dream-come-true.

From the moment they crawl off the hatch patch and into the bucket of blood meal below, the larvae get all their very favourite foods to eat. They get the sweet and the savoury in a two-course blend of culinary perfection – bran (the flaky kind; if it's too powdery they can suffocate), mixed with blood meal. The larvae that will be allowed to pupate and become the next generation of breeding stock get spoilt on human-grade food – no blood, just milk powder, yeast, brown sugar and bran. But, whether they are destined for adulthood or protein production, the larvae all get fresh air, climate control and 24-hour entertainment in the troughs that they call home. Clearly, the Larva Shed isn't a heaven where maggots go after they die. Rather, it's where they go to live the good life.

'For the larvae, blood meal is like the playground at a McDonald's where kids go to play. They burrow in and around in there. They can have fun while they eat.'

'For the larvae, the flaky bran and feed mix is like the playground at a McDonald's where kids go to play,' says Research Manager Gloy. 'They can have fun while they eat. The heat they generate makes a kind of hard, dry crust on top with their microenvironment underneath. They burrow in and around in there ... it's like playing with their food.'

But it's not all fun and games. Everything is optimised for maximal maggot survival and growth. 'There needs to be good ventilation,' says AgriProtein CEO Drew. 'The constant nutrient breakdown leads to ammonia build-up that could compromise air supply. We also need to watch the temperature. All the squirming, feeding larvae generate masses of heat in the buckets. It can get up to 45° or even 47°C in there, which is pretty hot for anything.'

Yes, larvae can survive at a range of temperatures. But 46°C is a life-threatening red zone for many living organisms. Research has shown that, at a temperature of about 35°C, the time to pupation is about three to four days, meaning a large number of third-instar larvae can be produced in just a few days. The third instar is the biggest, plumpest, most protein-dense stage of growth. Keeping the shed in a state of eternal summer is good for larvae and good for business. That said, earlier instar larvae seek out temperatures between 30° and 37°C, but just before pupation, they prefer a cooler 15°C. Similarly, larval light preferences also change with age. A physiological feature that can make maggot harvesting a much lighter job.

'The first-instar larva is negative phototrophic and moves away from the light, deeper into the breeding material,' Pieterse explains. 'As it reaches the third-instar phase it becomes more attracted to the light and just before pupation it moves to the drier, lighter regions. Harvesting can then be done by providing a dry area with the correct light intensity to the [third-instar] larvae. These larvae then move into this region and are harvested and dried.'

With the right food and temperatures, it takes about two to three days for the larvae to reach their perfect size. That's when they are ripest for harvesting. And, conveniently, by this time they have left the hot, moist heart of the bucket to go in search of the drier, cooler climes at the surface. Then you can simply pluck up the plumpest or, even more simply, just add water.

At harvesting time, the whole trough of larvae and bran mix is tipped into water. The larvae will float and can be skimmed off the top, like cream.

The whole trough of larvae and bran mix is tipped into water. The larvae will float and can be skimmed off the top, like cream. Finally: the *crème de la crème* of all forms of fly. The larvae have reached their richest and most valuable state. It's the pinnacle of their protein-growing career. From here, there is nowhere to go but down. And down they go, frozen and then dried to a slow but painless death. Unless they are the chosen few left to pupate.

THE PUPAE

If the temperature is at or near the ideal 35°C, pupation happens three and a half days post-hatching. That's less than a day after the ideal harvest time. Which explains why some of the larvae manage to sneak into pupae before they can be sent off to become protein. The flies that emerge from these pupae are accidental and incidental. They fly aimlessly around the Larva Shed like lost members of another generation.

But there are some planned pupations in the AgriProtein process. They are a necessary link in the chain – a step towards generating more adult flies for breeding. The larvae that are left to pupate are harvested straight from the troughs. These pupae are placed in the fly-breeding cages – where each kilogram of pupae will hatch into 12 million flies in three to five days.

Pupation probably isn't the most efficient part of the fly life cycle. Large numbers of the pupae are duds that lie lifeless on the floor of the cage and don't yield adult flies or anything else. But this is natural – or at least natural selection. There are still enough fruitful pupae to generate sufficient flies for the breeding to continue. And five to six days later, once the flies have reached sexual maturity, there are eggs again. And on it goes.

WHAT THEY GET OUT

One subzero day is all it takes. After a stay in the freezer, the cold-snapped larvae are defrosted, placed on drying racks and then slowly dehydrated in a dryer for 24 hours. Like a cake needs to dry. A frozen, dried, baked, protein larvae cake that smells chocolaty, like carob. Really. It smells tastier than it should.

Once the carob-scented cake is dry, it's broken into pieces that are crushed and milled into meal. Ladies and gentlemen, we have reached our destination. This is Magmeal. The brown, crumbly, crunchy, sustainable protein of the future. It's a good place to be. Even the scientists are saying so – a 2008 study by researchers at Rivers State University, Nigeria, has shown that larvae meal boasts a well-balanced wealth of nutrients, including around 55 percent protein.

This is Magmeal. The brown, crumbly, crunchy, sustainable protein of the future. It smells chocolaty, like carob. Really. It smells tastier than it should.

Clearly, Magmeal is the climax of the AgriProtein tale. It's the gold spun from thread or a prince sprung from a frog. Firstly, it's an complete animal protein, meaning it contains all nine essential amino acids, unlike plant proteins such as soya, which need to be supplemented before feeding to monogastric animals. Secondly, tests performed by the Animal Sciences Department at Stellenbosch University have shown that Magmeal leads to more weight-gain and less stomach strain than other industrial feeds.

It was tested on chickens. Thousands of chickens that were also a proxy for fish. Chickens, incidentally, are quick breeders with short lifespans – that's what makes them excellent research subjects, just like flies.

In short, the chickens liked it. This was confirmed by the amount and type of weight they gained per kilogram of food consumed. It was also confirmed by the way they ate it. Voraciously. Happily. Hungrily. Repeatedly. In addition to cohesion rate (or effect on body weight), Magmeal tested very well when it came to toxicity scores and gizzard erosion (GE) scores. Simply put, if a chicken gets an eroded gizzard (or an inflamed stomach) from a feed it won't thrive and probably won't want to eat it at all. This is more likely with foods that aren't a natural chicken choice. It's all very logical: in the real world, chickens don't eat fish or soya. But they do eat maggots. So their GE scores are better and the chicken gizzards win.

FLIES, FARMS AND THE FUTURE

Fly farms are like hen's teeth. Both are rarities. The stuff of fairy tales, urban legends and the wow-I-can't-believe-it dinner party conversation. Until recently, both have also been unlikely to develop. Mostly because there hasn't been any real use for them.

Unless hens suddenly develop a taste for biscotti or betel nuts, they will probably remain toothless and this is how things will stay. Fly farms, though, aren't so static. Our mutating modern world is constantly presenting new and urgent uses for places where flies are produced in swarms. In most cases they are fruit fly swarms destined for the Sterile Insect Technique (SIT). Bred by the millions or billions, male fruit flies are irradiated and sterilised before being released into the wild to mate unsuccessfully with wild females. It's like recruiting an army of eunuch flies to control populations from within. The result? Fewer fruit flies feeding on farmed fruit. It's a copulation cul de sac and a multi-billion dollar industry worldwide.

More than 25 centres around the world are pumping out various species of fruit flies in clouds.

In fact, there are more than 25 centres around the world pumping out various species of fruit flies in SIT clouds. In Guatemala alone they are raising 3.5 billion flies a week. That's a massive number of flies to put in and still get fewer out in the end. But, illogical arithmetic aside, SIT remains one of the most ecologically friendly methods of pest-control around. It is innovation and exploitation combined – an innovative way of exploiting one of the natural things that flies do best. Namely, mate.

Another thing that flies do best is eat, and get eaten. More specifically, they eat dead animals and get eaten by live ones. It makes sense that another form of innovation and exploitation rests on these very natural behaviours. But the innovation is driven by the need – the new and growing need for a sustainable protein source to feed the animals we humans want to farm and eat ourselves. There are some smaller-scale needs met by small-scale projects – like farmed flies sold as exotic pet bird feeds for around $80 a can. But, as our oceans are emptied of fish and our cities are filled with an ever-increasing number of people, the need for large-scale larval protein production is becoming more urgent by the day. Although, frankly, the word `urgent' doesn't sound urgent enough. Perhaps we should call it `crunchy'. It's a so-called protein crunch that makes the credit crunch look like much ado about nothing much at all.

Yes, running out of money is unfortunate and inconvenient. But fishing the ocean dry is a global disaster with ecosystemic effects. How do we make the situation a little less dire? Firstly, by facing up to the hard facts about what we feed our animals. And secondly, by feeding them something different.

It's a so-called protein crunch that makes the credit crunch look like much ado about nothing much at all.

That's where fly farms like AgriProtein come in. At this facility in the winelands of South Africa, research and development is driving ever-more targeted action. New production systems and fly families are being tested. New larvae are being created with unique chemical and mineral contents – designer proteins that deliver just the right nutrients to animals of particular ages. As the farm grows, so will its ability to supply the bulk animal feed industry. The flies are laying, the eggs are hatching, the larvae are squirming, the Magmeal is flowing out in bags. The business is buzzing, literally.

If this book proves anything, let it be that flies are not pests, but pioneers in our modern world. They make medical miracles and inspire aerodynamic design. They set fashion trends and travel in space. They amaze, entertain and give us something to hunt down and feed to carnivorous plants for sport. But none of this is going to save the world. Nutrient recycling and fly farming just might. It's a fairy tale in the making. But the "happily ever after" depends on us.

Yes, the fly is the hero of the tale. But this hero can't save the world alone. We humans have to help the fly. We need to build more sustainable farming operations. We need to fill our shopping carts with greener produce and a lot more thought. The crunch is coming, sooner than we think. Our fish stocks are already dwindling. Certain species are already rarer than hen's teeth. But hopefully things will change.

Our hero needs a sidekick. Question is, is it you?

BIBLIOGRAPHY

While only two key reference books were used in the research for *The Story of the Fly*, there are hundreds of obscure references in academic, online and other publications too numerous to mention. The key fly-related websites and resources are listed below:

Printed Sources

A Fly for the Prosecution: How Insect Evidence Helps Solves Crimes, M Lee Goff, 2000, Harvard University Press, ISBN 0674002202

Economic Entomology in Agricultural & Medical Perspective, Dr SK Ghosh and Dr SL Durbey, 2010, IBDC Publishers, ISBN 978-81-8189-472-4

Encyclopedia of Entomology, John L Capinera, Springer

New Scientist 1731, D Bickel, 1990

Principles & Procedures for Rearing High Quality Insects, John C Schneider, 2009, Department of Entomology and Plant Pathology, Mississippi State University, ISBN 978-0-615-31190-6

The Blue Economy: 10 Years, 100 Innovations, 100 Million Jobs, Gunter A Pauli, 2010, ISBN 978-0912111902

The washing away of wrongs: Forensic Medicine in Thirteenth-Century China, Tsung Tz'u, 1981 (current translation), ISBN 0892648007

Online Sources

Agricultural Research Council South Africa, www.arc.agric.za

Biomimetic Millisystems Lab, UC Berkeley, http://robotics.eecs.berkeley.edu/~ronf/Biomimetics.html

BioTherapeutics, Education and Research (BTER) Foundation, www.bterfoundation.org

Blue Economy, www.community.blueeconomy.de

Diabetes Care, http://care.diabetesjournals.org

Flies and Pesticides, www.pestproducts.com/flycontrol.htm

Flies in Agriculture, www.agriprotein.com

Flies in flight, www.flypower.com

Food and Agriculture Organization of the United Nations, www.fao.org

Forensicmed.co.uk, www.forensicmed.co.uk
Genetic Pest Control, www.oxitec.com
Genetics, www.genetics.org
InterSpace News, www.interspacenews.com
Journal of Cosmology, http://journalofcosmology.com
Journal of Environmental Biology, www.jeb.co.in
Live Science, www.livescience.com
Microbiologist, Society for Applied Microbiology, www.sfam.org.uk
NASA Science, http://science.nasa.gov
National Geographic News, http://news.nationalgeographic.com
Nature, www.nature.com
Pest Control, www.flycontrol.novartis.com
Proceedings of the Royal Society B, http://rspb.royalsocietypublishing.org
Sanitation Ventures, www.sanitationventures.com
Science Daily, www.sciencedaily.com
US Department of Agriculture Food and Nutrition Information Center, http://fnic.nal.usda.gov
World Health Organization, www.who.int
Wound Care Information Network, www.medicaledu.com

OTHER WORKS

The Protein Crunch – Civilisation on the Brink, Jason Drew & David Lorimer, ISBN: 978-0-9869976-2-4

Coming soon:
The Story of the Wind – and How It Could Blow Us Back on Track: Jason Drew & Justine Joseph

Praise for *The Protein Crunch*:

'The one book on the environment everyone should read' -- **Robert Swan, MBE FRGS, Polar explorer**

'*The Protein Crunch* is extremely timely and important, and it is also clear and convincing. It should be read by everyone who is concerned about the sustainability of the situation we have created on this small planet' -- **Dr E Lazlo, Founder of the Budapest Club**

'I found it full of fascinating information, well put together to constitute a kind of manifesto or warning for the future. Think differently, or see our society and its precious environment go horribly wrong' -- **Sir Crispin Tickell, GCMG, KCVO, President of the Royal Geographical Society, London**

'*The Protein Crunch* provides an excellent summary of all those systemic linkages regarding food, energy, water, land use and population, with plenty of pointers as to how to change course even at this very late stage. I can only hope that it will seriously affect the way people see our world!' -- **Jonathon Porritt, CBE, Founder, Forum for the Future**

'Fascinating links between seemingly unconnected things.' -- *The Sun* (UK)

'A motivational and remarkable book.' -- *The Mercury*

'One of our most inspiring green leaders.' -- *Leadership* Magazine

'Takes the complex and sometimes abstract notions of the environment and brings them down to earth with a bang.' -- Little Green Mag

'It's a while since I've read a factual book that has made me think so much.' -- *Burton Mail* (UK)

'If ever there was a book that smacks you into global awareness or drives you into denial, this is it.' -- Don Pinnock, *Getaway* Magazine

'Jason tells it like it is – and it ain't cosy.' – *Country Life*

'There's plenty of food for thought and fodder for dinner party conversations in this book.' -- *Cheryl Madhouse Reviews*

'Jason Drew is a Renaissance Man ... deeply knowledgeable and passionate about saving our world.' -- Sue Grant-Marshall, Radio Today

'Brilliant and fascinating.' -- Saskia Falken, Heart Fm

'Never before have I been so inspired and educated in the notion of thinking out of the box regarding real business sustainability and its effect on our world.' -- Kim Hickley, TSiBA (Tertiary School in Business Administration, Cape Town)